Dearest
Michelle,
Thank you for ...
Melanie

Cancer:
What Next?

Melanie Bone, MD

HEALTHY LEARNING

ISBN: 978-1-60679-111-0
Library of Congress Control Number: 2010928182
Cover design: Brenden Murphy
Book layout: Studio J Art & Design
Chapter page graphic: Dynamic Graphics

Healthy Learning
P.O. Box 1828
Monterey, CA 93942
www.healthylearning.com

I was shocked by the pathology report. The cancer was much bigger than any of us had imagined. Instead of 1.8 centimeters it was 6.8 centimeters, about the size of a small grapefruit! Also, more lymph nodes were involved. This meant chemotherapy and radiation therapy for me.

A few weeks later, I was ready to start chemotherapy. While I was in Gainesville, Florida, with my then-husband at a law school party 21 days later, my hair fell out. The pillow was covered, and the drain in the bathtub got stopped up from all the hair. I hid in the hotel room until it was time to go home. By the time we reached Palm Beach a day later, I was ready for the last bit of hair to be shaved off. My surgeon came over with her dog clippers. We put a chair in the driveway, and in minutes I was bald. The kids started shrieking that I was ugly and demanded that I put on fake hair. I began to cry. The denial was starting to crack. I wanted to salvage the situation, so I suggested a dip in the swimming pool. Then, I explained that I couldn't wear a wig there. Within a few minutes, we were splashing around. My children started rubbing my head. After that, they really never said anything about my baldness.

I think I have trained my brain not to remember too much about the next few months. Suffice to say that I survived the chemotherapy even though it was a rough time for me and my family. My treatments were finally over in February, and radiation started soon thereafter. April 10, 2001, was my last day of treatment. I started on tamoxifen, a pill to combat estrogen in the body, and launched into survivorship.

Now, almost 10 years later, I cannot believe I am still here, going strong. But I am. Cancer gave me a gift. I am touching more lives than ever with my story.

Introduction

I am Melanie Bone, a mother of four and a wife, a gynecologic surgeon, and a cancer survivor. Through this book, I hope to become your friend and help guide you, your loved ones, and friends through their unique cancer experience. This book will be your quick introduction. Feel free to read it in order or skip around to a chapter that interests you. Each chapter includes columns from "Surviving Life," a weekly column that I write for the *Palm Beach Post*. Some of these columns contain questions and answers because every other week I do a "Dear Abby" of cancer.

I also suggest that you visit my website (www.DrMelanieBone.com) to find what is here and much more. Read the "Surviving Life" columns not included in this book. Search the Q-and-A tab devoted to entertaining questions about cancer, big and small, common and less common. Submit your own private questions, too. Read blogs and testimonials about other people's cancer experiences, and feel comfortable sharing your own. Even find the perfect gift to give a cancer patient.

With half the population predicted to get some type of cancer by the year 2040, all of us will be touched directly or indirectly by this disease. Even if you are not the patient, you may have a family member, a friend, or a work acquaintance who is newly diagnosed or going through treatment. When I had breast cancer in 2000, I was surrounded by help—excellent doctors, my family, wonderfully supportive friends, and my precious children.

Still, I lay awake at night, afraid. I knew that nobody could have the surgery for me; nobody could take the chemotherapy or radiation on my behalf. And, nobody could take away the scars or the ongoing anxiety that the cancer might come back at any time. Being a doctor made it worse. I knew too much. I understood that my chances were 50/50 at best.

When I found myself alive five years later, I realized that I'd spent too much time afraid. My fear inspired me. I decided to devote my life, not to finding a cure for cancer, but to ending the fear of cancer. Why? Because too many of us see cancer through other people's eyes. The fact is that most of us survive our cancer. In many ways, cancer has become more like other chronic illnesses. Take diabetes, for example; after the shock of diagnosis, a patient begins a regimen of proper eating and may need to add oral medication or insulin over time. The disease is controlled, not usually cured. Why is it that more people are afraid of cancer, which is often cured, and less afraid of diabetes, which is rarely cured? The same is true for heart disease. More people die of their first heart attack, but people fear being told they have heart disease far less than cancer. The answer lies in the power of six letters: C-A-N-C-E-R.

Each and every one of you can help me take the stigma out of those six letters (C-A-N-C-E-R) that turn lives upside down every minute of every day. Don't face this alone, uncomfortable, and in discomfort. Find comfort in knowing that you are not alone, and eventually most of us will be able to sympathize and empathize without fear.

Now, turn the page to find out, each step of the way, what is next in each person's unique path through, and likely beyond, cancer.

1

Before Diagnosis

What is always speaking silently is the body.
—Norman Brown

There are two common ways that someone is diagnosed with cancer. Some people are diagnosed when undergoing routine screening. They have no idea anything is wrong. They find out about their cancer as a result of those screening tests. Other people have a complaint and are diagnosed after a medical evaluation.

Screening tests like mammograms, colonoscopies, and yearly prostate exams are designed to find cancer before it is symptomatic and when it is most curable. Most of us never really think these routine tests will really show anything because most of the time they don't—which is the reason that unforeseen diagnoses hit so hard. Common examples of this type of diagnosis include:
- Finding a cancer at a routine colonoscopy
- Finding a suspicious mass on a mammogram
- Finding a prostate mass on a rectal exam

In each case, the patient is not suspicious that they have anything wrong. When cancer comes out of the blue, it is a lot like a car crash. No preparation. Damage could be small or big, but the accident itself is only the start.

Not all cancer diagnoses are unexpected. Many people have a sixth sense about their health. They feel that something is wrong. A nagging pain, weight loss without trying, or a chronic cough may bother them, but they push it off as stress or "too much going on at work." Then comes a point when the physical ailment is just too intense to ignore, or pressure from family and/or friends forces the patient to face the problem. When those patients arrive on the doorstep of a doctor, they are less surprised to find out about their cancer. Some people actually are relieved to find out that they were not imagining the symptom. While nobody wants to hear the words "You have cancer," sometimes they provide a much-needed answer.

Some cancer syndromes run in families. Knowing your family's cancer history is very important. It can help your health-care provider to figure out if you are at risk of developing certain cancers. If so, then you will be able to have more close surveillance and hopefully earlier detection. For example, certain breast and ovarian cancers occur because of an inherited genetic alteration called the BRCA genes. Patients with suspicious family histories can be tested, and if they are found to have BRCA, they can elect to have annual mammograms and MRIs, and they can take medication to help prevent both breast and ovarian cancer. Other hereditary cancers occur, but you must see an astute physician and ask to have the doctor assess your personal risk.

Patients at risk for cancer who are not proactive might lose an opportunity for early detection or prevention. Then, they have to undergo many treatments that could have been avoided. I see it like this: if there is a bullet headed your way, and you know it, you can put on a bulletproof vest or move aside. If you don't know it, the bullet is still on the same path, yet you won't know to get out of the way. Knowing your risk of cancer is the same as looking for the bullet.

* * *

Sixth Sense: Intuition and Cancer

Women's intuition…it serves us well. And there are just as many men who have it as women who don't. How often do we make a decision based on a gut feeling? It doesn't mean that we ignore facts. Rather, intuitive people use a combination of objective and subjective information to make judgments. I think it happens all the time with cancer. To everyone else's eyes, I was the picture of perfect health. I'd just run a half marathon and was down to my "fighting weight." The day I went in for my biopsy, I looked into the mirror and saw a sick person. My cheeks were a bit too hollow, and my eyes were a bit too tired. Somehow, I knew.

How much importance should we give to hunches or intuitive impressions? Are we looking for a wild goose chase that way, or are we going to find that many cancers were right under our noses, and we minimized their symptoms out of fear of being diagnosed?

It seems my patients fall at the extremes of the intuition spectrum. Either they are so in tune with their bodies that they notice every minute change and worry each one is a sign of cancer. Others don't pay attention to even obvious growths until they can no longer ignore them. But where do we draw the line between intuition about one's own health and hypochondria? Following are a few guidelines to help distinguish between the two. The goal is to not subject patients to too many tests and yet not miss a cancer diagnosis by ignoring a complaint. Invariably, we make a few misjudgments, but with time, both patients and medical diagnostic testing improve.

Weight Loss Is Important

When the scale keeps dropping for no apparent reason, it deserves an evaluation. Of course, some people don't eat well under stress and lose weight. If the weight loss is accompanied by changes in bowel habits, it should raise a red flag. When a patient with lifelong constipation suddenly starts to have diarrhea and goes down two pant sizes, I first congratulate her on her new look; then, I rule out the common causes of bowel changes such as lactose intolerance, irritable bowel syndrome, or infection. If none of these turns up as the cause, I suggest a colonoscopy to look for colitis or cancer. I have patients who waited to seek medical care until they have dropped 30 pounds and can barely eat anything, or have dark blood in their stool for six months before they report it. A good rule of thumb: any spontaneous weight loss with new intestinal changes that last more than six weeks merits a visit to the doctor.

Fatigue

Fatigue is another complaint that can be caused by anything from stress to medication to cancer. It is such a common complaint with so many causes that even doctors don't agree on when and how to evaluate it. Many people don't sleep well when they are stressed or depressed, and either medical or psychological problems may be the root cause. This insomnia-based fatigue should resolve on its own or with a short course of a mild sleeping agent. Viruses like mononucleosis can make a patient so tired they cannot even get out of bed for weeks at a time. These conditions also resolve spontaneously. A good rule of thumb: persistent fatigue that keeps a patient bed-bound and unable to work or engage in activities that he usually considers fun should raise a red flag. Medical consultation should be sought in those instances.

Erectile Dysfunction

For men, erectile dysfunction is common, and prostate cancer, unfortunately, is also common. Although I am not a urologist, I do believe that some men must intuitively know there is a problem. It may be a change in their urine stream or the frequency with which they have to urinate. Some may develop impotence as a physiologic manifestation of their fear of prostate cancer. Perhaps it is the way their brain forces their body to go to the doctor. They develop the sexual concern as a foil. For many men, this is the only path to diagnosing their cancer.

Bloating and Gassiness

Women with bloating and gassiness may seem to be a dime a dozen to many doctors. However, some of them have pelvic cancers. In particular, ovarian cancer and fallopian tube cancer (and the same type of cancer called primary peritoneal cancer can be seen in women who have already had these organs removed) can present as a swollen belly with nondescript gastrointestinal complaints. It behooves women not to ignore these complaints in themselves as a part of normal aging. And it behooves doctors not to ignore these complaints in women, especially those that are postmenopausal and those for whom these are new problems. A short trial of dietary changes can rule out lactose intolerance and wheat allergy. Colonoscopy and/or endoscopy certainly can assess the bowel from the inside. If all these are negative, then these patients deserve an evaluation to be sure they don't have ovarian cancer. Every day, patients arrive at my office asking for a CA125 and a sonogram because they are sure they have ovarian cancer based on their bloating. Some of these patients will be right. It is my job to determine whose intuition has served them well to notice these symptoms and whose intuition is about to lead us on a wild goose chase. It takes a lot of my own intuition to figure it out.

Headache

What about misleading symptoms? Take headache, for example. Most headaches are caused by sinus infections or allergies, muscle tension, or migraines. However, I see many patients who are convinced their headaches are a sign of a brain tumor. Without a CAT scan or MRI, they cannot feel comfortable. I agree to schedule these tests, in part, because I personally understand the value of a negative scan. In the world of managed care and medical finances, it can be hard to justify spending medical dollars to prove that a cancerous condition doesn't exist. The relief afforded by a negative scan can actually save money. Why? Because patients develop more symptoms when they are worried about cancer. When their fears are allayed, they feel healthier, and many symptoms go away.

So it is always a fine line…paying attention to subtle symptoms versus ignoring nuisance problems. Even the most intuitive people can screw it up. My own intuition delayed my diagnosis. I ignored pretty obvious signs of my disease for months before I was diagnosed with cancer. Then, the night before I went in for surgery, I took one last look at my chest. I almost cried when I saw the skin overlying the cancer. It was dimpled like an orange peel. In medical school, this finding—called *"peau d'orange"*—is shown to students to learn about how to diagnose cancer. It happens because the tumor pulls at the skin from underneath, causing the little pore-like changes. My professors taught me that it wasn't that common to see it anymore since most cancers are found before they are advanced enough to cause *peau d'orange*. When I saw it on my own breast, knowing that I had first noticed something wrong almost six months before, I felt embarrassed and ashamed. I was mad at myself for not having intervened earlier because…somehow, I knew.

SURVIVING LIFE

Diagnosis by History

A lovely woman was in last year. Her chief complaint when scheduling the appointment was that she began to bleed on Thanksgiving after more than a year without a period. The bleeding alarmed her. She searched the Internet. A website advised her to seek medical attention, indicating bleeding that long after her last period was possibly a sign of a problem. Intelligent, calm, and an excellent historian—this was my ideal patient. The bleeding was preceded by sore breasts and the low back pain that she normally associated with her period. She thought her menopause was over because all the hot flashes and night sweats went away a few weeks before the bleeding. Her pelvic exam was normal, and my in-office sonogram confirmed no suspicious findings. My nurse drew hormone levels, and sure enough it seemed that after a year her ovaries had decided to "wake up" and cause one more period to happen. We waited a few months and rechecked her levels. She went right back into menopause, complete with hot flashes, flushes, and night sweats, and to date has remained there.

Recently, another woman with the same complaint of post-menopausal bleeding came for an evaluation. She also was able to give an excellent history. She had no typical menstrual symptoms before this bleeding and no change in her hot flashes. Actually, she was one of those blessed individuals who never had them in the first place. Her exam revealed no worrisome physical signs, but her sonogram confirmed a thick uterine lining. I did a biopsy of her uterus, and she had early uterine cancer.

Yet a third patient came in with the identical complaint of symptomless post-menopausal bleeding. New to my practice, I took an extensive history before examining her. She reported an abnormal pap smear a few years before. This made me suspicious of a cervical problem. Sure enough, an exam showed a tumor on her cervix. A quick biopsy confirmed cancer.

All of these patients point out a very important issue in diagnosing cancer. I was able to make an educated guess about each of these patients merely by taking a thorough history and doing an exam. The high-tech sonogram and the biopsy confirmed my suspicions. It reminds me that some doctors have forgotten the art of listening to the patient, touching them, and putting the whole picture together to make a diagnosis.

For my readers, it is a reminder that knowing, not ignoring, your body is key to being diagnosed with benign or cancerous conditions. Keep track of what is normal for *you* so that any changes are obvious. While it is easy to order a $3000 scan to find a cancer, think of how much money our economically strapped country could save if patients reported significant changes in their health *and* if doctors listened better to help make diagnoses. Ironically, the most common complaint I hear from colleagues is that they don't have time to spend listening to patients because reimbursements from insurance companies are too low. They need to increase their volume just to maintain their income. But, if they stopped ordering too many expensive tests and relied more on their eyes and ears, medical costs would go down, which could eventually increase their reimbursement. In fact, to encourage more low-tech medicine, some insurance companies track doctors' per-patient expenditures as a way to reward "more efficient" physicians. (Admittedly, this system is fraught with discrimination against doctors whose specialty requires using more expensive testing on a regular basis. It also can't distinguish between doctors who attract more complex patients and, as a result, need to do more testing.)

If we find a way to make patients better historians and doctors better listeners, we might diagnose the same cancers at a fraction of the cost. In medical school, I distinctly remember a great professor telling me that 90 percent of the time you should be able to tell what is wrong before leaving the exam room. That sage advice is the backbone of the way I practice medicine.

SURVIVING LIFE

❉ ❉ ❉

Unexpected News

The other day, a 70-something-year-old patient came in for her annual exam. She was in a rush to get out to do her holiday shopping. She wouldn't even let the nurses weigh her or measure her height. I started the exam, and when I got to the thyroid gland, I felt a large mass. As it turns out, she knew she had it, and she was told by a specialist that it wasn't anything to really worry about. When I got to the breast exam, I felt not one, but two masses. Both her mother and grandmother had breast cancer, but I don't believe she really thought she was at particularly high risk for the disease. My dilemma: Do I insist that she go for more testing immediately, or do I let it slide until after the holidays? What if my diagnosis of probable cancer is wrong? Then, I really ruined her day for nothing, and I look like an alarmist. If, on the other hand, it is a cancer, then I am both the heroine and the villain—the former for having made the diagnosis, and the latter for having made the diagnosis. For me, the situation was a bit of a lose-lose.

I felt pretty certain and went with my instincts. A sonogram was arranged the same day, even though her mammogram was read as completely negative one month before in another state. The radiologist called me while she was still there to say that he was certain one of the breast masses was a cancer and that the thyroid mass might be another.

Most doctors don't give a cancer diagnosis over the phone, but I felt my patient wanted to know the answer, good or bad. Waiting until after the holiday to tell her face-to-face would probably not have destroyed her holiday, but it would have left her fretting the entire time. It was postponing the unavoidable.

In the end, I did ruin her holiday. I called to tell her the diagnosis just two days before Christmas. She began sobbing uncontrollably. Her reaction to the cancer news was a combination of the gut reaction almost every person has to the diagnosis and the fact that it was so unexpected. In retrospect, I am not sure I made the right choice to tell her. If I'd waited to schedule her scans until the beginning of January, it would not have changed her outcome, and it would have made for a much nicer holiday.

✳ ✳ ✳

There are two points to remember: First, the earlier cancer is diagnosed, the more likely it is to be cured. Screening tests are designed to find cancer before there is a symptom. On the other hand, if you have a problem, it is not a good idea to ignore it. Forgoing health care only delays the inevitable in the case of cancer. Remember, most cancers are very treatable and even curable. Don't let fear prevent you from seeking help.

2

Denial and Anger

*Each difficult moment has the potential
to open my eyes and open my heart.*
—Myla Kabat-Zinn

Denial is usually what happens to cancer patients when they are first diagnosed. What is denial? Denial is the way our brain adapts to the news that we have cancer and lets us go on. When first hearing about a cancer diagnosis, it can feel unreal. Many patients report that they feel normal or that they feel that they might wake up and find out it all is a bad dream. These factors are a part of denial. Denial is a filter to lessen the impact of stronger feelings that lie beneath. It does *not* mean that you actively are denying that you have cancer. It does *not* mean that you are going to refuse treatment. Instead, it serves a very important purpose. Denial helps cancer patients to put meals on the table for their family and go about the business of daily living without falling apart. Sometimes, denial is so strong that family members don't want the patient to know the diagnosis or vice versa. They feel they are protecting their loved ones by keeping it a secret.

SURVIVING LIFE

* * *

Should Cancer Be a Secret?

When an elderly patient came in complaining of difficulty holding her urine, I was ready with a few possible diagnoses; perhaps a urinary tract infection or a dropped bladder. In medical school I was taught that 90 percent of diagnoses are made by history, so I ask a lot of questions to help me figure out the problem even before I touch the patient to examine her. Is there burning or frequency? If yes, I look for infection. Does it happen with cough and sneeze? If yes, I look for bladder dropping. Is there pressure or bloating? If yes, I look for a cyst or tumor pushing on the bladder. My patient wasn't the best historian, but I got the impression that the leakage was just happening regardless of how full her bladder felt or her need to urinate. Then I examined her, and the diagnosis was clear as day. A hard mass was sitting right there pressing on the bladder. Trying not to alarm her, I suggested a pelvic ultrasound. As a joke, I told her I wanted to be sure she wasn't pregnant, and her laughter eased the tension. Within seconds, I confirmed my worst suspicions: cancer.

After assuring her that there was no pregnancy there, I segued into telling that there was a growth and it needed further evaluation and probably surgery. "Do you think there is an easy cure?" she asked hopefully. Translation: "Do I have cancer, and am I going to die?" Obviously, she had a clue that there was a really serious problem. On the other hand, her husband had told me before the visit that she had a mild memory loss, so I wasn't sure how best to address the problem. I asked her to dress and come into my office to discuss the situation, and then had my nurse bring her husband back before the patient joined us. We chatted while his wife dressed. I quickly explained my concern that she had ovarian cancer and asked his opinion about it. He thought it best not to tell his wife the truth, but to keep it from her. He expressed concern that she was too fragile to take the impact of the news. He was so afraid for her that he wanted to shoulder the entire burden himself.

A few minutes later, the three of us sat together, and I tiptoed around the subject. Was I obligated to tell her the correct diagnosis, or respect the fact that the man who had loved her for more than 40 years felt that I should not? I started using words like "tumor" and "mass" and "exploratory surgery." She nodded in a very innocent way. Then, out of the blue, she looked right at me and said, "I guess I have cancer." So much for keeping it a secret. Her husband started sobbing. She covered his hand with hers. That gesture said so much. It said: "I know you are thinking that I am going to die of my cancer and leave you alone after all these years, and there is nothing you can do to prevent it."

Years ago, it was common not to tell patients about their cancer. When there were no good options for cancer treatment, giving the diagnosis was the same as offering up a death sentence. Doctors tended to be paternalistic. It was commonly believed that the patient would have less of a will to live if they knew they had a terminal illness, so instead of including the patient in their own health-care decisions, the patient was kept in the dark. They were "kept comfortable." The family waited for the patient to die. Sometimes, this happened quickly; sometimes not. I remember a friend telling me that her mother went to the doctor complaining of a breast mass. She went in for a biopsy and woke up having had a full radical mastectomy. She took to her bed for six months, waiting to die. Still alive six months later, she got up. Decades later, she is still alive and well.

Nobody wants to be the bearer of bad news. The word "cancer" has so much power that most doctors dance around it. Luckily, every day there are advances in early diagnosis and treatment of most cancers, and many cancers are curable. Wouldn't it be nice if one day the word cancer was as scary as the common cold? Then, being diagnosed and treated wouldn't be as traumatic. Certainly there wouldn't be a need to hide the diagnosis if the norm was a good prognosis.

Is it just the fear of dying that encourages us to hide cancer? I am not so sure. Maybe it is the perception of the torture of treatment followed by long-term suffering with a less-than-optimal chance of survival. But just having cancer, even curable cancer, has a stigma associated with it. The cancer patient can be the nicest person in the world, and people become afraid of them. Some friends stop calling, both because they do not want to catch the patient at a "bad time" and because they are uneasy about conversing with a cancer patient.

They become pitied, even if they do not feel pity for themselves. Personally, I remember friends looking at me with sorrowful eyes, as if I had already died, when I wasn't even finished with chemotherapy. I felt a strong urge to force them to look directly into my eyes and tell them that I wasn't about to die. No, I was prepared to be around for a long time.

Now, I realize that choosing whether or not to keep cancer a secret is really the patient's decision. It is completely unfair of a doctor or a family to decide for the patient. Besides, most people with cancer know they have it. Trying to fool them about it is an exercise in futility. The secret, if revealed in an unexpected way, can irreparably damage a relationship. No matter how weak someone claims their spouse, parent, sibling, or friend may be, hiding a cancer diagnosis is not doing the patient any favors. Back to my sweet patient, she is finished with surgery and chemotherapy. Not only does she not hide her cancer, she has become a poster-child for ovarian cancer awareness in her adult community. Never underestimate the positive power of this disease.

* * *

Denial can continue for a long time. Some patients or their family members worry that the patient hasn't had a breakdown since being diagnosed. For those patients, denial is strong. It is not necessary to force the issue. Eventually, it will come out; but maybe not for a long time. For me, denial lasted throughout my treatments. It reared its head for a second when I lost my hair, but came back right after as I bravely kept my social commitments with a big smile. It was very important to me to show a good face. Breaking down was not an option. I have talked to many other cancer patients who feel pressure to maintain a positive attitude during their cancer and feel like a failure if they don't. Those feelings are all manifestations of denial.

My denial ended later when I started to examine my whole situation. Just when I was starting to feel better physically, I figured out that my personal life was not what I wanted it to be, and my denial melted away. I let myself understand that my marriage was unhealthy and was preventing me from moving forward in my life. It was then that I started appreciating the potential positive value of a cancer diagnosis.

Other common reactions to a cancer diagnosis are anger and its counterpart, depression. I have seen patients scream, fall down and have an old-fashioned temper tantrum, and then start blaming all the bad things in their life as the cause. Sadness sometimes expresses itself as anger and vice versa. This emotion is hard for doctors, patients, and their families to handle. After all, nobody is comfortable around a mad person. Best not to overreact or feel that it is your responsibility as a spouse, other family member, friend, or colleague to reason the patient out of it. Better to just quietly support and let them let their feelings out.

✳ ✳ ✳

Cancer and Depression

"You have cancer." I can't think of many other three-word sentences regarding your own health that evoke such an intense visceral reaction. When I heard those words, I was under the influence of anesthesia drugs, and it still didn't soften the blow. I was lying on a stretcher in the surgical recovery room when my teary doctor leaned over me and told me. I remember feeling like the world was coming to an end, but not being able to express much because I was numbed by the medication. Over the next few hours, it hit me harder and harder. There was mild shock (I had guessed the diagnosis before surgery), anger, disbelief, and overwhelming depression. I started taking antidepressants soon thereafter. They did not take away my sadness, but I was able to get out of the house to go to doctors' appointments and treatments while taking them. My oncologist also had me see a therapist who specializes in dealing with cancer patients and their families. Talking with her helped as much, if not more.

My experience was very typical. That is: discover you have cancer, get depressed, and start treatment for depression with medication and therapeutic counseling.

Recent studies confirm what would seem fairly obvious. Cancer patients have a higher likelihood of being depressed. Makes sense. Another study showed that patients with highly-aggressive cancers and little hope for a good long-term outcome had more depressive symptoms than those with stable disease and less-aggressive cancers. Patients with passive personalities showing a less aggressive nature, tended to have a more fatalistic approach to cancer and their "given-up" attitude translated into shorter survival. Also makes sense. These studies were done *after* the diagnosis of cancer was made.

I read a theory that some depression comes before cancer. So which comes first: the cancer or the depression? In one particular study, major depression happened more frequently to men who were destined to develop pancreatic cancer. How did they figure that out, you ask? In a study of 749,000 persons in Iowa and South Dakota, it was found that about 10 percent had a mental disorder. Of those people, 2 percent developed cancer. In contrast, of the 90 percent that had no mental disorder, 0.02 percent developed cancer. Further study showed that, for men, there was a correlation between developing pancreatic cancer in the aftermath of depression. Since that study was done using cases dating back to 1989 to 1993, there have been more studies done, looking into an association between depression and cancer. Some prospective studies show a link between depression and developing cancer, but others do not.

If depression is related to getting cancer, what would be the mechanism? There are theories that people with repressed anger, internalized stress, and anxiety may have a predisposition to cancer. But why? It may be that the immune system and/or the endocrine system are involved. We call this the mind-body connection. It makes logical sense that our mood may alter changes in our corticosteroid (or stress) hormones and vice versa. These adrenal hormones may affect the immune system, which, in turn, may hamper our natural ability to rid ourselves of the cancer cells that our bodies make every day. Depressed people may be deficient in certain natural cancer-fighting cells, which may make them more predisposed to cancer. At this point, the data are not entirely clear, and many physicians (me included) are concerned that it could be harmful for patients who are depressed to be told that they are more likely to develop cancer. We must await the results of more definitive research.

Antidepressant use also complicates the picture. While these drugs have saved millions of lives, they may be implicated. A few articles relate their use in depressed patients to an increased risk of cancer. Some studies have shown that certain antidepressants can stimulate tumor cell growth in the laboratory setting. These findings will not necessarily translate from lab into office, but again, more research is needed.

Research takes time and money, and it struggles to keep pace with the ever-changing environment. At this point, I believe we are still pondering the chicken-egg controversy. The same may be true for the depression-cancer relationship.

* * *

Over time, these intense feelings fade a little bit, especially when patients need to move on to understanding more about their specific diagnosis. This leads to the next step—information seeking.

3

Information Seeking

The period of greatest gain in knowledge and experience
is the most difficult period in one's life.
—Dalai Lama

No matter how cancer is diagnosed, the first question that comes to mind is "What next?"

Whether by phone, face-to-face, or in writing, there is no easy way to tell someone they have cancer and no easy way to receive the news. Why? Because both patient and caregiver probably have the mind-set that the "c" of cancer leads to the "d" of death. Remember, we are here to change that.

I routinely tell my patients their diagnosis over the phone for a few reasons. First, they are usually in the comfort of their own home. Their reaction is private. They don't have to stop at the checkout desk to pay a co-pay or bill and then drive a car to get home. I figure this is safer. Second, they might also be in the presence of loved ones whom they would not bring to the office to console them. If a doctor tells you to bring a spouse or other family member with you, it is almost like telling you over the phone anyway. Lastly, most of the counseling I would give to a patient face-to-face is forgotten before they get up out of the chair. They usually need the whole situation explained again when they are not in shock.

I start off by advising the patient to grab a pad and pencil and write down the most basic facts that I need to relate to them. I spell the out the type of cancer and advise a website for basic information. Then, I schedule a visit in the office within the next day or two and recommend that they bring someone with them, usually a spouse, sibling, parent, or friend to act as an advocate…and to remember that pad and pencil with their questions on it.

What happens next is predictable. Patients hang up and boot up. Some less computer-savvy patients head for the library. This starts the phase of information-seeking. The Internet is a great resource, but some of the information found there would more accurately be called misinformation. Sticking to major sites such as the American Cancer Society and the National Cancer Institute is a good idea. Talking to your father's Aunt Sadie, who had a horrible experience with chemotherapy, is not. While family and friends with cancer experiences are more than happy to share them, I suggest that the patient not listen to any of them. Remember, cancer is not one disease. There is not one cure. Each person has the right to their very own, unique cancer journey. Every step of the way will be people, well meaning people at that, who try to make the patient travel down their cancer path. This really is not appropriate. It may take minutes, hours, days, or even weeks, but most become highly educated about their cancer, sometimes to the point that they may try to dictate their care.

SURVIVING LIFE

Should Patients Force Cancer Testing?

Remember the days when you went to the doctor and he examined you in one room (and there were fabric cover gowns). Afterward, when you were dressed and sitting in the doctor's personal office, the doctor sat down and talked with you. The conversation sometimes moved to family news, because the doctor was often a friend and took care of your mother and father, sister, brother, and Uncle Al, too. You were asked about how you felt and what might be worrying you. Only then did a nurse come in to draw blood. Some time later, the doctor would call back and tell you everything was fine or, if not, you were sent for a few more tests. Patients didn't know the exact numbers of their blood work, and they would never dream of telling the doctor what blood tests they wanted or thought the doctor should order for them.

That was called "old-fashioned" medicine. Patients trusted their doctors. That scene still takes place, but not nearly as often. For one reason, there has been such an explosion of medical knowledge that one doctor can no longer keep up with the latest developments in a numbers of areas. Thus, the specialist. By dividing medical care into a series of specialties, there is a greater chance that each specialist can continue to practice state-of-the-art medicine. To compare to the mundane: if there were only one car dealership, it would be unreasonable to expect the salespeople to discuss the intricacies of the Audi, the Saturn, the Honda Element, and the Aston Martin with knowledge. Individual dealerships opened to specialize in certain car types. The analogy applies across the board to shoes, construction, banking, and so forth, but I digress.

Now, general medical doctors and specialists alike are on the receiving end of laundry lists of tests patients think they need (or someone on the Internet suggested). What is a doctor to do? Tell these very informed patients that they should go to medical school before trying to practice medicine? Very tempting sometimes, but a definite road to disaster. Spend the time educating these very intelligent patients about the nuances of testing and the intricate thought processes that lead up to the decision about which tests are best suited to that patient? Too time consuming and all too often frustrating. So, we give in. We do tests we are not convinced are necessary, but probably are not harmful. We feel defeated, but giving in can be so much easier than trying to save medical dollars. "Above all, do no harm" is the oath we took in medical school. Nothing about economy of health-care dollars. Most of us agree that we cannot afford to pit our concerns about medical economy against Mr. Smith's demand for a mercury level (or whatever test is in question). If we don't give in to the request, he will seek care elsewhere with a caregiver willing to draw the test. And if, on the extremely tiny chance that he is right, and we denied him the test, we become responsible. Next thing you know, we are in a courtroom, defending our actions in a malpractice suit.

This situation has brought about a new breed of doctors. They are young enough that they barely remember old-fashioned family doctors. They are smart, understand tests and computers, and many don't know much about talking to patients, let alone touching them. Some doctors skip the physical exam or postpone it until lab tests are back. Their argument is that the blood-test results will afford them a clue of what areas are of concern. I understand that. But I also think that it might lead them to skip over symptoms or signs that could be a result of medical problems not best diagnosed by bloodwork. Not all doctors are guilty, but some visualize the patient as a CBC, abnormal EKG, elevated PSA, and such. Cancer, in particular, has a lot of numbers and tests connected with it. While these can be vital to deciding patient care, they can be confusing and misleading as well. So let's review the pros and cons of a few commonly demanded tests.

CA-125 (Cancer Antigen 125)

CA-125 is a blood test that is controversial, even among doctors. It was identified by Dr. Robert C. Knapp when he was searching for a way to diagnose ovarian cancer at an early stage. The test looks for a certain marker that is found on the surface of cancer cells. Because CA-125 is not specific to ovarian cancer, it is not a good screening tool. It can be elevated when there is no cancer and can be normal when cancer is present. The Internet is awash with stories of women who were diagnosed with a pelvic cancer and are convinced that they would have had a very different outcome if only their doctor had ordered a routine CA-125. Almost every gynecologist I have ever met will tell you of multiple patients who pressured them to order the test. When it came out elevated, the doctor was then obligated to do sonograms and/or CAT scans that were unrevealing. A good number of these patients actually ended up with surgery, including a hysterectomy, because once the test was elevated, the patient couldn't find peace, even with negative scans. They felt certain they were brewing a cancer that was just not big enough to be seen or too subtle to appreciate even on the most sensitive tests. Lo and behold, the overwhelming majority of these patients had perfectly normal organs taken out of them. "Questionable" surgery may not seem that terrible as an intervention for elevated CA-125, but sooner or later, a patient who demanded a CA-125 which led to a "questionable" hysterectomy will die of a complication of surgery such as a blood clot. The doctor doing the surgery must be able to look into the mirror and feel she was doing the right thing for the patient. Luckily this outcome is a rare happening. Ironically, the more common scenario is that the patient has a repeat CA-125 after the surgery, and it is *still* elevated. Bottom line: It is rare that a mild-to-moderately elevated CA-125 as an isolated finding (without any complaints on the patient's part or any abnormality on a scan) is a sign of cancer. On the other hand, this test is an excellent way to follow ovarian cancer patients *after* their treatment. Until it can be improved or a new test developed, it is not a good test to draw based on patient demand.

PSA (Prostate Antigen)

Unlike CA-125, the PSA is a blood test done on men yearly after the age of 50 to detect prostate cancer. This test is excellent to find prostate cancer if it is elevated. However, it is the year-to-year change in each patient that can be as important. For example, if the test was 0.7 one year and then 2.1 the next, it could be worrisome, even though the values are both in the normal range. Unlike the CA-125, the PSA is very specific for the prostate gland. It can be elevated in the presence of a prostate infection, so not all abnormal values mean cancer. The PSA should also be done in conjunction with a prostate exam. The combination of an elevated test and a palpable prostate nodule is highly indicative of prostate cancer. The PSA can also be used to follow patients after their treatment. Most men note that their PSA plummets after surgery and/or radiation therapy. If the PSA starts to go back up, the treating doctor will evaluate for a recurrence of cancer.

CEA (Carcinoembryonic Antigen)

This test is done to look for colon cancer. It is valuable, but not a substitute for a colonoscopy.

HCG (Human Chorionic Gonadotropin)

HCG is the name of the pregnancy hormone. It is the one that we look for in the urine when performing an over-the-counter pregnancy test. It is sometimes used in cancer. There is a cancer that develops from the placental tissue, and it produces HCG in extremely high levels. This cancer, called gestational trophoblastic disease, is responsive to an aggressive, multi-agent chemotherapy regimen. It is very treatable, even at later stages. This tumor blood test is a great way to follow patients unless they get pregnant; then, the problem is that the test will skyrocket, and the doctors can't be sure if this result is because of the pregnancy or the cancer.

LDH (Leukocyte Dehydrogenase), CA19-9 (Cancer Antigen 19-9), CA15-3 (Cancer Antigen 15-3), AFP (Alpha-fetoprotein)

The list of tumor markers and antigens goes on and on, and every day more letters are added to the alphabet soup. Some come in to vogue for a time and then are discovered to be not specific enough. The goal of research is to find markers that are very specific for a cancer and also very sensitive, meaning that it can detect that cancer early, at its most treatable stage.

I can almost imagine the day when we, the hands-on physicians, are obsolete. The patient will show up and have blood drawn and a body scan done. Only after the diagnosis is made will the patient then be referred to the appropriate health-care provider. Sound like a bad science-fiction movie? I really believe we are not that far away.

I am pretty sure it won't happen in my lifetime. Thank goodness, because I was trained in the old school. Many of my finest diagnoses were made while looking for subtle, non-verbal cues from a patient during the history and physical exam. And I don't believe that any amount of blood or scanning can improve on that.

✳ ✳ ✳

By the time I have scheduled a follow-up visit to discuss the next steps, my patients are ready with excellent questions. Admittedly, some are still so overwhelmed that they have not done any self-educating, but that is a rarity these days. Unfortunately for them, the media frequently puts out "cutting-edge news" to sell their paper or show. Two days later, more news, completely at odds with the prior report, is reported with just as much intensity. Media medicine is all around us, but not always good for us.

✳ ✳ ✳

SURVIVING LIFE

Media Medicine

Every week, my mailbox is filled with "stuff." I am sure there are people who read all the "stuff" in their mailbox, but not me. I could probably save money if I paid attention to this mail, but my problem is that it is accompanied by a steady stream of medical "stuff." Since I don't have time to read them all, I pay more attention to the medical "stuff." I get coupons offering training to do office spa procedures like Botox® to generate more income. I toss those right away. Then I get "real" medical "stuff." There is a biweekly newspaper filled with up-to-date articles about obstetrics and gynecology. Two glossy journals with fetching cover photos entice ob-gyns to read up on their specialty to stay current. Finally, there are the real journals, thick and loaded cover-to-cover with technical articles about clinical studies and bench top research. These are required reading. After all, my job is to guide my patients responsibly through decision-making that will impact their health, and staying current in my specialty is a requirement, not a luxury.

Other doctors also work hard to maintain their knowledge base. But we lament a new phenomenon that erodes the value of reading journals and going to continuing medical education programs. Nicknamed "media medicine," it is the power of the press to present "breaking" medical news before doctors are aware of it. I open the paper and watch TV and am dumbfounded at how quickly the media is able to scoop a newly-published study before the scientific journal for that month arrives. More problematic is that they may hype a study undermining or reversing current practice. Remember Vioxx®? A great arthritis drug that many patients still miss. How about silicone breast implants that were "in," then went "out," and are now back "in" again? Not only is this practice a disservice to the medical community, but it negatively impacts the doctor-patient relationship by making doctors seem uninformed and leaving them to field large numbers of calls about an issue about which they are no better informed.

Patients march in with the latest medical information in the media and begin what I call the "confrontation consultation." Suddenly, I am being attacked for prescribing a medication that, to the best of my knowledge, is beneficial. Often the patient is worried about a rare risk associated with the drug that has only surfaced with widespread usage. Remember Fosamax® and osteonecrosis of the jaw? I have yet to meet a doctor who has seen a case, but many patients are demanding to come off the drug or switch after reading the articles in the press. It is no wonder that doctors are frustrated when patients refer to the *New York Times* as a source more reliable than an academically vetted journal.

While I am all for including patients in medical decision-making I believe there is a line between active participation and fully controlling the situation. Cancer patients, in particular, need to be their own advocates, but I see some trying to take charge of their own care based on superficial medical knowledge derived from the press. Instead of cooperation, there is defiance. The saddest part about this phenomenon is that it drives a wedge into the middle of the doctor-patient relationship. The need for patients to trust their doctors is essential for good outcomes. Nowhere is it truer than for cancer patients.

Breast-cancer survivors and women at high risk for breast cancer are bombarded almost daily with news-breaking medical information through the media. The recommended dos and don'ts seem to change from day to day. Estrogen-replacement therapy suffers from media medicine. Depending on which day it is, estrogen is either beneficial for almost every organ in the body, or it a major cause of breast cancer, heart disease, stroke, and dementia, or all of the above. While most of these women try to avoid taking estrogen for hot flashes, night sweats, mood alterations, and memory complaints, if they subscribe to the Suzanne Somers school of hormone replacement, then they will absolutely want it. When Ms. Somers faced questioning on *Larry King Live*, the lack of good scientific data behind her opinions was revealed.

Each doctor has his own approach to media medicine. Some will simply dismiss it and dogmatically state they know more than the newspaper or TV. Not a bad approach at times, but what happens when the media is right? Physicians using this technique are expressing their frustration that the patient doesn't trust them. The problem is that patients may misinterpret this behavior as arrogance, and this reaction causes friction in the doctor-patient relationship.

For those doctors with enough time, having an in-depth conversation with the patient is a great approach. It is then possible to determine where the patient obtained their medical knowledge and to teach them why a particular study may be flawed and not apply to them. Doctors are often maligned for failing to listen and discuss issues with patients. With poorer reimbursements and continuous pressure to see a high volume of patients just to maintain their income, doctors often point to these constraints as the reason they can't sit down to spend the time necessary to refute media medicine. Most doctors think through their decisions, but may not have the time to explain the rationale behind their decisions. Patients misconstrue this behavior as thoughtless or pedantic. I can't defend every doctor, but most of my colleagues consider their patients' needs and involve them in discussions about media medicine within reason.

Today, a new "throwaway" journal came, so termed because doctors read and toss them right away. It had an article about the benefits of moderate alcohol consumption in mid-life women as a heart-disease prevention strategy. I cringed. Just last week, there was a story in the papers correlating even minimal alcohol consumption with an increased risk of breast cancer. No doubt about it, my phone is bound to start ringing with calls from patients who read both and are confused. Maybe the media that came out with both stories should hire a medical professional to field all the calls from worried patients. Then the rest of us in-the-trenches docs might be able to appreciate all the other "stuff" in our mailboxes.

* * *

As a gynecologist, I find that one of the most important things I can do is to refer the patient to a capable and trustworthy oncologist and/or oncologic surgeon to begin further testing and treatment.

What comes next? Finding the right physician.

4

Finding the Right Physician

You can't make someone else's choices.
You shouldn't let someone else make yours.
—Colin Powell

Selecting the right physician or physicians to provide treatment is the next step in the cancer journey. I have seen just about every approach to this task. Some people scour the Internet to find the *best* doctor at the *best* institution to be treated. Others simply ask me to suggest a good doctor, and I do my best to refer accordingly. Deciding what is important to the patient factors into this decision. Is the patient someone who prefers a small, personalized place to be treated? Does the patient want input from multiple doctors at a cancer conference to discuss her case? Is the patient comfortable with a teaching hospital where students, interns, residents, and fellows will all be a part of her care? For me, staying close to home, near my children was one of the tipping points. Although a friend offered me her personal jet to go anywhere in the world to be cared for, I knew that feeling butterfly kisses on my cheeks and being in the tumult of my own home felt more comfortable than flying off to a major cancer center for treatment. Having said that, had I had a rare cancer treated only at one place in the country, I would have taken her up on her offer. Whatever the patients choose to do, it is really important not to undermine them. I know spouses who were so mad that the husband or wife elected to have their care at hospital A when they thought hospital B was better. This is not a battle. Letting a patient have autonomy and control over their disease is a part of ending denial and moving to what comes next: making the decisions about the nature of the treatments.

✳ ✳ ✳

SURVIVING LIFE

Referring the Newly Diagnosed Cancer Patient

Almost every day, I am asked to refer a newly diagnosed cancer patient to "the best" oncologist or surgeon. It is tempting to ask the patient what they mean by "the best" doctor, but I try to help them without professing to be certain that I know for sure.

Little do patients know that there is no such thing as "the best" oncologist or cancer surgeon. Many excellent doctors are available. What constitutes "the best" is a concept worth exploring.

There are physicians who work at medical facilities reputed to be "the best" in the nation. Should I refer to "the best" place, even if I know nothing about the doctor? If a university setting has fabulous statistics for treatment, but you as the patient are seen by the medical student, resident, fellow, and perhaps by the attending physician for only a split second, are you getting "the best" care? On the other hand, if you see a doctor trained at world-renowned facility, but who is no longer working there, is that person still one of "the best"? Sometimes.

Sometimes not. I get feedback that some of the best-trained doctors are book smart, but not clinically adept. Conversely, I have encountered doctors trained at "second-rate" hospitals who are incredible clinicians. While there is a tendency for doctors who are very skilled to have completed their internship and residency at top-notch programs, it is not absolutely necessary.

I also wonder, is "the best" doctor the one who is the best diagnostician, even if he is not the best at treating, or is "the best" doctor one who takes a patient already diagnosed by another physician and treats with unparalleled skill? For cancer in particular, diagnosing the stage is so important, because treatments are often by protocol based on stage.

Where does bedside manner fit in? If you believe, as I do, that the patient-doctor interaction is of paramount importance for treatment, then "the best" doctor may be the one who develops a wonderful rapport with the patient as opposed to one who has better technical skills. I remember picking a surgeon to do my mastectomies who was probably not on the top of other doctors' lists. I knew she really cared about me and would give 100 percent to see me get better. She was definitely the right surgeon for me. In fact, she told me she prayed that the cancer would be all gone while she was operating on me. It made a huge difference to me. I was impressed that she was so invested in my health outcome.

There are always patients who care about the essentials of the doctor-patient relationship, but there are some who are less interested in a physician who can do handholding. I do hear patients ask to be referred to "the best" surgeon and specifically tell me that they do not care about personality or rapport, mainly about surgical skills. What these patients can't know is that most of us do not operate with each other. As one doctor referring to another, we rely on reputation, patient feedback, and our own relationships with other physicians. I may be unsure exactly how well Dr. X does his surgery. I see the scars at a later date. I hear the patients describe how nice or not nice the office was and how accommodating Dr. X's staff was. But rarely am I in the room to be able to say with certainty that Dr. X does a better prostatectomy than Dr. Y.

I could opt to be paternalistic about my referrals and just give two or three names of colleagues who are well known. For me, that isn't the best way. I like to refer to a doctor who will keep me in the loop and give me feedback, involving me if there is a reason.

At the end of the day, we are fortunate enough to live in a country where the vast majority of board-certified doctors are competent to do the job. It is our perception that there is a "best," but as you can see, there are many "bests," and what is most important is that you, the patient, find "the best *for you.*" You can do this by listing what is most important for you. Is it place of training, bedside manner, technical skills, or access to physicians at other facilities for conferencing and advice? Once you are able to express your needs, then it will be easy to introduce you to the "*very* best for you."

Ultimately, it is the outcome that matters. If the patient survives the cancer, then the doctor did a great job and was "the best."

Best of luck…

✻ ✻ ✻

5

Treatment Decisions

As my awareness increases,
my control over my own being increases.
—Will Schutz

With the decision regarding the "best" doctor made, *what next*? Time to face treatment options. When deciding how to treat cancer, there are four approaches: not to treat at all, to use conventional treatments, to use alternative treatments, or to use combinations of conventional and alternative treatments, either together or one after the other. If you have a good rapport with your team of doctors, chances are you will agree on a mutually acceptable approach to treatment without much drama. On the other hand, if you distrust your doctors or if you are someone who can't shake off the perceived negatives to conventional therapies, alternative therapies, or both, it might take you a long time to decide. You must make peace about your choices. Ultimately, the outcome will determine if you made the right choice. And even if the choice was not "the best," usually there is an option to re-treat in a different way.

Some patients know exactly what they want regarding surgery and adjuvant therapies. They will control as much as they can. At the other extreme are patients who ask no questions and do whatever they are told to do. I was neither too pushy nor too passive. I knew that I had to have one breast removed so I decided to remove both at the same time. I figured it was the best way to avoid having to find myself in the same situation again. That was reason enough for me. After that, I let my doctors take the reins. When I picked my surgeon and oncologist, it occurred to me that if they'd come to me as a gynecologist to ask my opinion about treating irregular periods or pelvic pain, I wouldn't want them telling me how to do my job. I let my surgeon pick the plastic surgeon based on her experience operating with many different doctors.

The surgery was surprisingly easy to get through, maybe because I'd birthed four children in less than four years. My body had been through a lot. I'd been pregnant for almost five years straight.

Fourteen days after I had my surgery, I was able to attend "new parents" cocktail reception in anticipation of my oldest child starting kindergarten a week or two later. A week after that, I was ready for chemotherapy. The oncologist took over. She advised me to randomize in a study about chemotherapy. There were no placebo arms, just two different types of chemotherapy and different dosing intervals. I'd read that patients who participate in studies have better outcomes. To this day, my oncologist claims she gets more people to participate in studies when she tells them I did. When she suggested eight rounds of chemotherapy followed by six weeks of radiation, I only asked when we were getting started. Amazingly, I ended up randomizing to the dose and schedule I secretly wished I would get.

I still remember how scared I was on the first day of chemotherapy. I was shaking so much they had to give me strong sedatives just to keep me in the lounge chair. Then, I was given one tablet to take. The nurse told me it would prevent nausea and vomiting. I clearly remembered women having chemotherapy during my residency. It was so violent that they often ended up readmitted to the hospital with dehydration. It was really hard for me to believe that a little pill taken less than a half an hour before starting powerful chemotherapy would do the trick, but it did. I never threw up once during the whole time.

Was chemotherapy a walk in the park? No. But I came to know how my body would respond. The first day or two, I felt queasy and was a little hyperactive from the steroids they gave me. Then, four or five days later, I felt really exhausted. On those days, I didn't do much. I read, played on the computer, or watched TV. For me, not having to go to work and just being able to rest made a big difference.

For certain people, maintaining their regular schedule during chemotherapy is really important. They need to feel that cancer is not controlling them. Fine with me. When I was interviewed by *ForbesLife Executive Woman* magazine about working during treatment, I was the only businesswoman who decided that time off was the right approach. The others proclaimed that working harder both helped them to overcome their cancer and to prove to their colleagues that it wouldn't slow them down. Whatever approach a cancer patient takes, it needs to be respected and supported.

Most treatment for cancer still relies on the trilogy of surgery to remove the bulk of the cancer, chemotherapy to kill off cancer cells that might have spread to other parts of the body, and radiation therapy to control cancer cells that might remain in the area surrounding the tumor destined to regrow in the future. Unfortunately, these modalities attack both cancer and noncancerous cells in the body, which is why there are side effects from the chemotherapy and radiation therapy. Over time, researchers are trying to make the treatments more specific to the cancer cells. For example, immunotherapy that uses the body's own defense systems like a silver bullet to destroy only cancer cells is now available for certain kinds of cancer.

Everybody uses her own approach to getting through treatment. I am not fond of thinking about cancer as a battle, but there are some people for whom this is the best approach. Others use guided imagery, imagining a scene or a series of meditations to get through. Whatever your approach, trust in just getting through each day. If you have eight treatments, take each one as it comes instead of worrying about all of them at once.

Finding the right way to support a cancer patient can be hard. What feels good for one patient may be offensive to another. Friends might think pampering with a spa day would be a great, but it might not be appropriate during treatment. Immune compromise may put the patient at risk for an infection in a spa. Also, she may have scars that make skimpy dress in a spa uncomfortable, both physically and emotionally. Trust me, for many cancer patients, just doing the dishes, taking out the garbage, or doing a load of laundry is heaven on earth. Small acts of kindness translate into giant gifts.

How long does treatment and its fallout last? Depends on the cancer. Some cancers, like kidney cancer, are treated by removing the cancer. Follow-up chemotherapy or radiation is not done except in rare circumstances. Leukemia and lymphomas are often treated just with intravenous infusions or oral chemotherapy without much surgery, and there are children's cancers that are treated with at least two full years of infusions. Breast cancer, once out of the early stages, requires surgery, chemotherapy, and maybe radiation. Doctors want to minimize treatments and maximize results, even if it seems otherwise.

Hair loss still is high on the list of "what I hated most about cancer." For me, it made the cancer so much more real. Following are not only a few columns, but also some questions and answers that are typical of those sent to me by patients, families, and friends.

SURVIVING LIFE

✳ ✳ ✳

Hair

How often do you find someone who really loves her hair just the way it is? It is either too straight or too curly. Too long or too short. Too blonde or not blonde enough. Well, I was one of those rare individuals who really liked my hair. It was long, thick, and wavy. As much as I loved the hair on my head, I despised the hair everywhere else on my body. It, too, was long and thick. I was forever spending a fortune on waxing, plucking, and shaving to get rid of it.

Then came cancer. Everyone warned me that going bald with chemotherapy was the worst part. No matter how prepared you think you might be, there is nothing quite like the first time you look at yourself in the mirror, bald as a cue ball. You may have denied that you were a cancer patient until that moment, but there is no denying it when faced with that shiny scalp and no-eyebrow look.

I remember how brave I tried to be. I had a party at a salon owned by a friend whose first wife died of breast cancer. He was going to give me a short, sassy cut in anticipation of losing my hair. He opened his salon on a Monday for me. Anyone who chose to have their hair cut that day donated the money to breast cancer instead of paying him. We had food and drink and a lot of laughs. I left feeling exhilarated and pretty. Two weeks later, just 18 days after my first chemotherapy, I went on an overnight trip with my then-husband. He went to meetings, and I took a bath. When I let out the water, the bottom of the tub was covered with hair. The towel was covered with hair. The pillow was covered with hair. I couldn't believe that I still had any left on my head. I went out to a business cocktail party that night and spent the entire time petrified that I would shed the rest onto the floor or on some person's jacket as they passed by. The next day, we returned home. I had to do something. I called my friend, who was the doctor who performed my mastectomies. She loved animals and came over with the electric shearing device she used on her dog. We put a chair in the driveway, and in a matter of minutes, I had a shaved head.

My four children (ages 5, 4, 3, and 3) took one look at me and screamed in horror. I had warned them that I would go bald, but it obviously made no difference. The oldest told me to go put on "fake hair" because I was so ugly. She started to cry, I started to cry, and I was at a loss for what to do. I was still itchy from the hairs. I decided to go for a swim. The kids jumped into the pool with me. I explained that I couldn't wear "fake hair" in the pool, and they agreed. Within a few minutes, we were playing and laughing, and they completely forgot about my baldness. For the next year, it was their "new normal," and it was not an issue at home. Sometimes I would cover my head, and sometimes I wouldn't. The kids would often get into bed next to me and rub my head. They were showing love to their mother, and their mother didn't need hair to be their mommy.

Unfortunately, while I was at ease at home with being bald, I was definitely not at ease with my predicament outside of the house. I hated wigs. My head happens to be the size of a child's, and all adult wigs that I tried on were so big that they came down over my eyebrows and pushed my ears out. One hairdresser found me a petite wig, and I wore it when absolutely necessary. Most of the time, I used scarves and hats. I would tie a scarf around my forehead as both a cushion and a cover-up for the lack of sideburns and neck hair. Then I would wear a wide-brim hat over the top. I didn't fool anyone, but it was the best I could do. I didn't like baseball caps because you could see on the sides that I was really bald, and I wasn't a good enough scarf-tier to make great head covers. Over time, and with the help of a friend that worked at Hermes, I was able to tie my scarves so that on occasion I didn't need a hat over the top.

What about the other hair on my body? Well, admittedly, losing the hair on your legs is not a big deal. Losing pubic hair made me look pre-pubescent, and I felt that was a bit strange. Losing eyebrows was much more traumatic than I thought it would be, and losing eyelashes led to constant tearing. For the eyebrows, I tried pencils, but felt that I looked like some old movie actress way past her prime. I either arched them too much or too little. If I tried to make them thick, they looked bizarre. Too thin, and it looked like my three-year-old daughter had drawn them on. I ended up buying an eyebrow kit with stencils and powder. While not perfect, it was much better than my freehand attempts. I did feel embarrassed to whip out a plastic stencil to get my eyebrows on when I'd accidentally wiped one off with a tissue. On more than one occasion, I found myself in a ladies' room, staring at a one-browed monster. I was never sure when or how I'd lost the other, just that I did.

Finally, one day, during my radiation therapy, I felt some peach fuzz on top. It was either white, gray, or blonde; I couldn't figure it out. That bit was quickly overtaken by very dark and very curly hair. Sinead O'Connor I wasn't, but as soon as there was 1/8 of an inch, I went without head covering. I remember a trip to Washington, DC to lobby Congress about funding for breast cancer research. I went out to dinner for the first time without a hat or a scarf. I thought I would feel less awkward because everyone was a stranger. Wrong! I still felt all eyes upon me when we walked to our table. The other diners' eyes seemed to wonder if I was trying a very new fashion. It was not the best meal of my life.

Many other survivors told me to expect that my hair would be curly and very thick when it grew in. Curly? Yes. Thick? No. It looked like a brunette version of Little Orphan Annie. But it didn't last. I noticed that a year or two later, the curls were down to waves. I expected to go back to that wavy look I'd had my whole life. But it kept getting straighter, and it never got thicker. In fact, I now have a bald spot on the back of my head. My eyebrows never came back all the way either. I used to joke that I looked like Brooke Shields with a unibrow. No more. The woman who had always waxed me started coloring my eyebrows to make them look thicker. The eyelashes that came back are nowhere near what they used to be. Lucky for me that the Brazilian look is in because the same goes for hair "down there."

I grieve my permanent loss of hair. I look at pictures of myself 10 years ago and feel a twinge. I don't want to seem vain, but I miss the hair that was. There is one thing that makes it all seem okay. I figure that if the chemotherapy killed off those hair cells and they never grew back, then there is a good chance that the it did the same to the cancer cells in my body. I really don't know now that I have straight thin hair if it will change again. But it is my "new normal," and I try to be grateful that I am alive and able to remember all those "bad hair" days of the past.

* * *

SURVIVING LIFE

Letting Cancer Patients Take Control

Thanksgiving has long been my favorite holiday. Kitchen aromas fill the house. My grandmother's best china is brought down from the top shelf. The day is both exhausting and fulfilling. For me, it is the essence of family and motherhood.

This year is different. My children are going to be with their father, and my house floods have destroyed my dream for an at-home Thanksgiving. I haven't felt this way since Thanksgiving 2000, during my cancer treatments. That year, I was too sick to enjoy Thanksgiving. Food tasted like cardboard, and I was too tired to sit at the table and pretend to be social.

Maybe this year is designed to keep me humble. While the cancer memories fade, I don't want to forget them, because every day other people all around me are having that same experience.

Following are some suggestions for those of you who are cancer patients or who have a loved one undergoing treatment at this time:

- Plan your usual function, but don't put stress on the patient to participate. If she wishes to come to the table for a short time and then disappear, that is her right. Don't make a big deal out of the fact that she is there or that she leaves to go rest. Try to avoid the temptation to bring the patient a plate piled high. You might ask specifically what she wants and bring only that.

- Don't be hurt if she is apathetic or even cranky about it. She is feeling bad. Her appetite may be lousy, and her taste buds are off. She might be resentful that everyone else is enjoying the day. Most cancer patients expend a lot of effort trying to keep everyone around them feeling normal. It can only last so long. When they get too tired or feel bad enough, they may lash out at people around them. Give a wide berth. Perhaps you can make a plate, definitely not overloaded, and then wrap it up and store it to be reheated when the patient feels better.

- The temptation to make everything right and to bring back a tradition can be overwhelming. If you have a cancer patient in your family, the whole holiday can be uncomfortable. If giving up on your traditions is too difficult, there are alternatives. Get invited to someone else's house for dinner. Or order in. In either case, the cancer patient has the option to go or stay home and have a bite later on.

Whatever you decide to do, involve the patient in the decision-making. You may be surprised about her attitude. Whether she chooses to participate or not, support her unconditionally.

Whether today means turkey with all the fixings or a turkey sub from the deli, I am going to remember my Thanksgiving Day from 2000, bald and blah, and be immensely grateful that in 2008 I have a full head of hair and the energy to write a column complaining about my own choices.

Quest for Kinder Cancer Therapies

Dr. Susan Love, a world-famous breast surgeon, coined the phrase "cut, poison, and burn" to describe the typical cancer treatments of surgery, chemotherapy, and radiation therapy. Most of us who have experienced chemotherapy firsthand think of it as a rite of passage in the cancer world. The chemotherapy experience is terrifying from start to finish.

I remember going to my first chemo session. The room was freezing. I was shaking from fear and the need for a warm blanket. Memories of my residency, when I was the one administering the chemo as part of my training to be a doctor, flooded my brain. In those days, we admitted people to the hospital for chemotherapy.

Why? Because there were no super-effective medications for nausea and vomiting, so we needed to have the patients on intravenous fluids to prevent dehydration. I distinctly remember a young woman coming off the elevator in a wheelchair with an emesis basin tucked beneath her chin. Just the thought of getting chemo started her vomiting uncontrollably. While the doctor in me knew that the new medications almost eliminate vomiting, the patient in me was petrified.

The nurses gave me a cocktail, and before long, the famous "red devil" (Adriamycin®) was going into my body while I contentedly read *People* magazine. The actual infusion was not bad. The side effects took a few days to really hit me. Then, I felt like I was walking through a wall of Jell-O®. The chemo was so powerful that it killed all the "good" cells in my body along with the "bad" cancer cells.

My digestive tract was a mess. There were oral ulcers, stomach upset, and then constipation or diarrhea, depending on what drugs I was taking. My blood counts plummeted. This was a sign that the chemo was working, but it put me at risk for infections of all kinds.

Dr. McKeen, my oncologist (I owe my life to her), gave me a shot of Neupogen® to jump-start my bone marrow to make infection-fighting white blood cells.

She advised me to move out of my house for a short time. She felt my four babies posed a significant risk for me catching a virus. Lying on the floor of my friend's house, writhing in pain from the one-two combo of a flu shot and the Neupogen shot, I could only think that there had to be a better way to selectively kill off cancer cells without doing in the rest of body's "good" cells.

As soon as chemo was over, I pushed the experience way into the back of my mind, moved on, and didn't think about it for a long time.

Then, the other day, I received an e-mail from the Pfizer Corporation. Pfizer is an enormous drug manufacturer. Pfizer makes Aromasin®, Zoloft®, Viagra®, and a whole slew of other medications. What I did not know about Pfizer is the extent to which the company is involved in cancer drug development.

As a result of the e-mail, I had the opportunity to chat with Dr. Jean Beebe, its lead investigator for new cancer drug research and development. She was in Florida because Pfizer is teaming up with Scripps to do some of their research work in Palm Beach County.

Dr. Beebe explained that the number-one goal of chemotherapy drug development is to target cancer cells exclusively. This is harder than it would seem. Cancer cells can look and act a lot like the cells of their host organ in the beginning. Over time, as they grow faster and faster and make tumors, their behavior can change. The concept behind targeted therapy is to find a drug that will identify the cancer cell early and kill it without harming the nearby normal cells.

Currently, there are a few targeted therapies on the market. Herceptin® is one that many people have heard about. It is a monoclonal antibody. This means that it uses the immune system to destroy breast-cancer cells that have a special marker on the surface of their cells.

Herceptin is now given both in conjunction with standard chemotherapy and for years after chemotherapy to keep the cancer cells at bay. It can have some side effects on the heart, but overall it is considered safe.

Tissue growth factors are another area of new research and development. VEGF is a growth factor. It stimulates the growth of specific cells. There are now drugs targeting VEGF that do not wreak havoc on good cells. Drugs that prevent cancers from setting up a blood supply to support their growth are called neoangiogenesis drugs.

The drug Avastin® is now on the market for many cancers and works this way. Unfortunately, it has its own risks. It can lead to bleeding in unwanted places because it interferes with blood vessels.

Sadly, even if there are a lot of good ideas around, there are huge financial obstacles. Why? Because for every one or two drugs that make it to market, 98 to 99 drugs never do. The average cost to bring a new chemotherapy drug to market is $500 million to $1 billion. This number is so high because it covers the cost of testing all the drugs that never make it.

After speaking with Dr. Beebe for some time, I was encouraged that there are talented people thinking of creative alternatives to our current chemotherapy. I am sure that drugs like the "red devil" are going to be a part of our armament for some time. But I look forward to the day when I can tell my great-grandchildren that the treatment I had for my breast cancer was so old-fashioned, it can only be found in the history books.

DEAR DR. BONE

✳ ✳ ✳

Nausea and Vomiting

Dear Dr. Bone,

Isn't it true that chemotherapy causes horrible nausea and vomiting? I am petrified to have chemotherapy if I am going to be that sick. What can be done?

A.S.
Manalapan, Florida

Dear A.S.,

It is true that many of the drugs used to treat cancer cause nausea and vomiting. Luckily, amazing drugs are now used to treat the nausea and vomiting that is due to the chemotherapy. I remember in the 1980s, patients would be admitted for chemotherapy that is now done outpatient. The main reason was to control the side effects, mainly nausea and vomiting. One patient stands out in my mind. We needed to give her an emesis basin (a small bowl for patients who throw up) when the elevator doors opened and she saw the hospital corridor. She started to be sick just with the memory of her prior treatment.

Thank goodness that rarely, if ever, happens anymore. Medications such as Zofran® and Kytril® are amazing. Even given orally or as an instantly-disintegrating tablet, they can completely eliminate the nausea and vomiting associated with the most powerful chemotherapy agents. Also, bursts of steroids are used and help markedly. Many patients go through their chemotherapy without ever getting sick to their stomach.

If you are extremely anxious, perhaps your doctor can prescribe some mild anti-anxiety medication. It really can help take the edge off a very scary situation. My own doctors had to give me some because even I, the doctor myself, was shaking like a leaf on the day of my first chemotherapy. I found it much easier than I had expected, but the medicine helped enormously. Once I knew what to expect the next time, it made the whole experience easier.

Some of the medications given to prevent side effects from chemotherapy must be taken for a few days after. If you try to cut corners and stop them early, you might have some rebound nausea, so I suggest taking them as directed.

Dr. Bone

✳ ✳ ✳

Lost Eyebrows

Dear Dr. Bone,

I just lost all my hair during chemotherapy. This may sound dumb, but do you know if there are false eyebrows? I have a wig and fake lashes, but somehow, when I draw my eyebrows with a pencil, they look really bad.

NoBrow
West Palm Beach, Florida

Dear NoBrow,

I remember my no-brow days well. I used a stencil kit that I found online to help me draw on eyebrows. Instead of pencil, I used a taupe/gray powder which looked a bit more realistic. There were days when I got home and looked into a mirror to find I had only one brow—the other probably left on the sleeve of whatever shirt I wore that day or accidentally rubbed off on a tissue I used for dripping eyes and nose. While I am not aware of any good glue-on eyebrows, I think patience is your friend. They will grow back. And if they aren't as thick or dark as you want, you can then tattoo to fill in.

Dr. Bone

DEAR DR. BONE

Ports and IVs

Dear Dr. Bone,

My daughter was diagnosed with leukemia. She needs to have two years of chemotherapy, but the doctors tell me that she has an excellent prognosis. The oncology team suggests that she have a port placed. What is a port?

D.J.
Orlando, Florida

Dear D.J.,

Children's leukemias are an area of medicine that has evolved tremendously. My own first cousin died of leukemia about 40 years ago because there were not good treatments available. Today, he would have survived thanks to new protocols like the one they are suggesting for your daughter. The chemotherapy for these blood cancers usually lasts at least two years in order to get the best cure rates. Imagine having to get an IV that many times. Ouch! Even adults wouldn't like it, let alone kids. That is the reason they are suggesting a port. A port is an internal IV usually located in the chest just beneath the collarbone. A port can be placed either on the left or the right side. It looks and feels like a plastic button under the skin. That button is connected (also under the skin) directly to the large veins in your chest, using flexible tubing. When it is time to have a treatment, a tiny right-angled needle is pushed into the button and is removed at the end of the chemo session.

A port is placed under anesthesia and is tested right away to make sure it is working. If chemotherapy treatments are spaced apart or completed, the port needs to be "flushed" periodically to make sure it isn't clogged. This is usually done right in the chemotherapy infusion center or in the doctor's office. Eventually, the port is removed, often under local anesthesia in a surgeon's office.

A trick I suggest, especially for children with ports, is to use a numbing cream (EMLA is a popular one) before going in for treatment. Then, even accessing the port is not painful. The cream must be put on thickly with an occlusive (tight) dressing about an hour ahead of time for it to work best. Ask about getting a prescription for it before the next chemo.

Dr. Bone

Dear Dr. Bone,

I just got out of the hospital after being treated for a kidney tumor. There is a hard bump where my IV was. Is this normal?

D.V.
Palm Beach, Florida

Dear D.V.,

It sounds like you are describing a superficial thrombophlebitis. Thrombophlebitis is a long word for an area in the vein where the blood has formed a clot that is irritating it. The blood clot is firm, and it is usually tender. Most of these clots are not deep under the skin and pose no real threat. They are very unlikely to break off or travel anywhere, a complication that happens with deep, large clots. The typical IV-related phlebitis is best treated with hot packs. You can use a hot washcloth or soak the arm in a tub of very warm water two or three times per day. Some doctors may suggest taking a baby aspirin each day, but it varies from doctor to doctor, and you need to ask your doctor to be sure. If the skin overlying the area becomes hot or red, you should be sure to contact your doctor immediately. Otherwise, you can expect that the phlebitis can last for a few weeks. After the pain goes away, the bump slowly but surely shrinks until you cannot feel it any longer.

Dr. Bone

DEAR DR. BONE

Myths About Surgery Causing Cancer to Spread

Dear Dr. Bone,

Everything seemed fine with my husband until he had surgery for cancer. Right after that, his cancer spread everywhere, and he died. Then, somebody told me that the operation caused the cancer to spread. I can't sleep wondering if that is the case.

R.R.
Jupiter, Florida

Dear R.R.,

First, let me offer my condolences on the loss of your husband. While it sounds like the operation caused the cancer to spread, it was more a case of timing. You didn't mention what kind of cancer your husband suffered from, but there are many cancers that are found quite late in their natural course. When the surgeons operate, they encounter widespread disease that was probably about to make itself known anyway. The actual act of surgery has not been shown to increase the likelihood that a cancer will spread. Cancer surgeons are trained to do all they can to prevent the disease from spreading, including taking out healthy tissue around the cancer (called "getting clean margins") and removing or assessing the lymph nodes that drain cells from the area of the cancer. Sometimes, there are clean margins, but the lymph nodes contain microscopic amounts of cancer. This raises the chances that the cancer will reappear because once the cells are in the lymph system they can travel. Incidentally, that is why many cancer patients will be given chemotherapy even with clean margins as insurance against any cells that may have escaped and already be starting to grow in other parts of the body.

Dr. Bone

Cancer and Weight Gain

Dear Dr. Bone,

Since I started chemotherapy for my breast cancer, I have gained 15 pounds. I thought cancer patients lost weight and were skinny. What gives?

T.L.
Palm Springs, Florida

Dear T.L.,

Many cancer patients come to diagnosis because they are losing weight without trying. The weight loss is probably due to the fact that cancer cells use up a lot of calories when they grow fast. Another reason for weight loss in cancer patients is decreased appetite. Sometimes this happens because taste buds are damaged by chemotherapy, and food doesn't taste good anymore. In terminally ill patients, the loss of appetite is called cancer cachexia and seems to be part of the body's shutting down in preparation for death.

Weight gain during cancer treatment is common. Most oncologists use steroids as part of the chemotherapy pre-treatment. The steroids reduce nausea. They also help to prevent allergic reactions to chemotherapy. Steroids are only given short-term and can't really explain all the weight gain of cancer patients. Another reason for weight gain is stopping dieting. The diagnosis of cancer is all the excuse they need to stop dieting. This goes hand-in-hand with weight gain from depression, a condition that is almost universal in cancer patients. Patients are depressed and have no will power. Their drug of choice to treat their blues is food. Finally, women undergoing cancer treatments can find themselves too weak and tired to do exercise. Weight gain happens when more calories are taken in than are used up. If the patient doesn't change what they eat, but stops exercising or just increases their caloric intake slightly, they gain weight.

Good news. You can lose the weight. Start slowly. Add a little exercise, and decrease caloric intake by about 200 to 300 calories a day (one candy bar), and you will lose two to three pounds a month. That's 25 pounds in a year. You can do it.

Dr. Bone

DEAR DR. BONE

Energy Levels During Treatment

Dear Dr. Bone,

I started chemotherapy about two months ago and have noticed two things: I gain weight and feel hyper right after my treatment. I even cleaned the house at 2 a.m.! I thought I should feel worn out, but the tiredness comes on the second week. Why is that?

Nightowl
Boynton Beach, Florida

Dear Nightowl,

I suspect that your oncologist is giving you steroids such as Decadron® as part of your pre- and post-chemo regimen. These medications are designed to prevent nausea and diminish some of the side effects of chemotherapy. Two side effects of steroids are fluid retention and increased appetite—both reasons for weight gain. Some people experience an increase in energy and activity level. I remember not sleeping well. Although I didn't clean my house in the night, I did get up to read and watch TV at all hours. Eventually, I asked my doctor for a medication to calm me down at night, and it helped. Luckily, these side effects are transient, and you will most likely lose the weight and slow down when you are finished with chemotherapy.

Dr. Bone

✳ ✳ ✳

The Red Devil

Dear Dr. Bone,

What is the "red devil"? My sister is scheduled for chemotherapy this week, and the nurses told her that it is the nickname for the drug she is going to get. Why is that?

S.S.
Tequesta, Florida

Dear S.S.,

The drug you are referring to is called Adriamycin®. The nickname comes from the fact that the color of the medicine is red. It looks like Jell-o going into the patient's vein. The reason that the word devil is associated with the medication is that it is very strong and causes intense fatigue and other side effects. Nurses must wear special gloves when handling it because it is so toxic. The good news is that it is a very effective cancer treatment. I believe I am here today thanks in part to my friend, the red devil.

Dr. Bone

✳ ✳ ✳

As I mentioned at the start of this chapter, some patients desire alternative or integrative treatments. For them, the question is, what next?

6

Alternative Treatments

Just as muscles become stronger and bigger when they work against resistance, so our minds and spirits enlarge by meeting the difficulties life presents.
—Andrew Weil, M.D.

To use or not to use alternative treatments, that is the question. Most cancer patients consider using something the doctor did not prescribe, either because a family member or friend told them about it, or they learned about it in the newspaper, on the Internet, or through TV or magazines. The list of complementary medications is so long that entire books have been written on the subject. I hear patients complain that their doctors are not well-versed in alternative treatments or object to them out of hand. I explain that doctors cannot all be walking encyclopedias. Oncologists have a huge amount of medical information to study, let alone stay current on alternative treatments. In medical school, they were taught that treatments not been proven by testing with randomized, controlled, double-blinded, prospective trials are not reliable. Most non-traditional therapies have not been scrutinized that intensively. These types of studies take years to do and make it almost impossible to establish the efficacy of a treatment before another comes along.

Doctors' tendency to "poo-poo" alternative treatments also results from the enormous choices available and the lack of safeguards against fraudulent products. Most oncologists, just like any other person who is not familiar with a proposed treatment, advise against it. Why? The Hippocratic Oath taken by physicians states "Above all, do no harm," and we take that seriously. Also, there is a fear of getting sued if something goes wrong when using a nonstandard therapy. Like conventional medicine, the state of the art changes all the time, and it is virtually impossible to stay abreast of conventional medical oncology literature and alternative cancer literature simultaneously. Please don't mistake your doctor's disinterest in mushroom extract as a negative sign.

If you are interested in eschewing traditional care in favor of alternative (meaning non-conventional treatment) or using complementary medicine (in addition to conventional treatment), you may need to seek out what is right for you. The Internet is full of questionable websites, so I suggest looking carefully at multiple sites. I did. Chemotherapy can be hard on your liver. I read that milk thistle is good for liver support. Milk thistle is an herb used in Europe to treat hepatitis and other liver toxicity. There does not appear to be harm in taking milk thistle. As soon as my chemotherapy was done, I started taking milk thistle. To this day, I take it every morning. I am not sure if it is helping, but it has become a habit. My doctors know I take it, and most do not comment on it. Other herbal supplements don't impress me as worthwhile. Other people may feel differently, but each of us has a limit. Shark cartilage is a good example. It was touted as an unparalleled anti-cancer substance by believers. Over time, shark cartilage has not been shown to be harmful, but it does not seem to have the potency it was thought to have.

Some alternative-therapy manufacturers and websites rely on people telling their story about an amazing cure to sell their products. We call this "anecdotal medicine." Sometimes, the findings prove true. Other times, they don't pan out. Every patient must find her comfort level with conventional, alternative, and complementary medicine.

Patients in dire situations tend to look for alternatives as a last straw. Told by their doctors that have failed all traditional interventions, they are vulnerable to claims of miracle treatments and must be careful what they try.

I know that complementary medicine is here to stay and look forward to the day when all cancers are treated with an integrative approach.

✳ ✳ ✳

SURVIVING LIFE

Chaga: The Mushroom of Immortality

Tonight, I attended a kosher eco-vegan seder. I never knew such an entity existed. It was fabulous. The dinner was a vegan celebration of the Jewish holiday of Passover. For those who don't know, vegans do not consume animal products: no poultry or fish, and no dairy derived from an animal (such as goat cheese or milk). The meal was overseen by Rabbi Loring Frank, a vegan himself, and was attended by fascinating people. Very spiritual. Very healthy. On the long drive home from Ft. Lauderdale's vegan restaurant, Sublime, where the event took place, I had time to contemplate becoming a vegan. If I weren't so into moderation, I might try it. The delicious recipes full of healthy fruits and vegetables tempt me. Many vegan recipes feature mushrooms, one of my favorite foods. This line of thought led me to remember an email I received about an amazing mushroom.

Mushrooms have gotten a lot of press over the past few years. It turns out that the humble fungus has many medicinal properties. Reishi and shiitake mushrooms are touted as having immune-supporting and anti-cancer properties, but they are not as powerful as chaga. Both a reader and a friend introduced me to this miraculous mushroom, and if even half of its proposed benefits are real, I would agree that it should be in our drinking water.

Chaga has been around since the 16th century. It grows wild in Siberia and northern Asia. This wild variety is the best. It is a black, irregular fungus that is found on the side of the birch tree. The scientific name for it is *Inonotus obliquus*. It is also known as cinder cork because it looks like a piece of burnt charcoal on the side of the tree. The chaga mushroom is commonly made into a tea in Russia, and Eastern medicine practitioners have been using it for centuries to balance a patient's "chi" or vital energy.

How does chaga treat diabetes, infections, hypertension, and cancer? The answer lies in its many special components. First, the mushroom is high in beta-glycans. Beta-glycans are immune modulators. They act to enhance our immune function, which enables the body's defenses to be stronger. Second, chaga has a high super-oxide dismutase (SOD) content. SOD inhibits free radical oxidative reactions, which are the basis of so many diseases, from wrinkles to cancer. Chaga helps to repair micro-damage to our genetic material, DNA. This is important because DNA breaks lead to cancer. Perhaps with the right help, DNA damage can be reversed and repaired before it causes disease. Chaga contains betulinic acid derived from the birch tree. Betulinic acid is drawn into the center of tumors and causes pre-programmed cell death to occur. Chaga also is naturally colored by melanin, which can be beneficial for health and has vitamin D2 precursors in it.

I couldn't find any chaga toxicity issues, just some comments about the purity and strength of the mushroom harvested. It seems that only a handful of the chaga mushrooms found in the wild are really qualified to be harvested—like truffles. There are not many rigorous scientific studies available to prove the efficacy of chaga, but there did not appear to be a lot of negatives to it either. The FDA has approved it as a "food," which means that it can be sold without the same degree of testing that it necessary for a medication to make it to market. The most well-known research was conducted at the University of Helsinki. I checked the National Cancer Institute, and there was no mention of chaga, nor was there anything at the National Center For Complementary and Alternative Medicine. It does have a few nicknames that must relate to prior successes: The Mushroom of Immortality and The King of Herbs, to name a few.

My friend started taking chaga and reports more energy, sharper thinking, and better sleep. Sounds good to me. The downside to chaga, as I see it, is that it is a multi-level marketing system (MLM). While I'm told that MLM is a way to raise capital in these difficult times, I think it makes products more expensive and less available. With automatic delivery, shipments are made on a regular basis and products go from factory to your home without sitting on a shelf in the health-food store, where they might go bad. I know good products get to market through MLM, even ones I support and use, but somehow the MLM basis of chaga leaves a bad taste in my mouth. By the way, the chaga doesn't. It is odorless and tasteless. Even children can benefit, and you can sneak it into their sippy cups. It comes as a liquid with a dropper, and you take 10 to 40 drops a day depending on your need—and your pocketbook. At about 60 dollars a bottle, it isn't for everyone—just those that take their health and longevity seriously.

As a cancer survivor who worries that her DNA may go awry again at any moment, I have nothing to lose. I'm going to order a bottle tonight and try it. Maybe I'll go back to the vegan restaurant and see what mushrooms are on their menu.

SURVIVING LIFE

Protocel

My father, a true Renaissance man, is an 81-year-old retired psychiatrist. His tastes are eclectic as reflected in our home decor. In my childhood, the basement playroom was decorated with antique medical memorabilia. Early in the morning, I would creep downstairs and read some of the framed stories. I loved the one about a 40-pound tumor taken out of an unsuspecting woman who complained of a stomachache. Dad really enjoyed collecting unique medical stories along with old advertisements for compounds and "snake oil" elixirs.

Recently, I heard about a compound called Protocel® (also called Cancell®). I searched for it online. There are many websites about Protocel, and they reminded me of my father's basement collection. The compound is supposed to be the most powerful antioxidant known to man. Websites are replete with amazing testimonials about how patients who were at death's door, given up on by their own oncologists, are now doing great without any signs of cancer years later just by taking Protocel.

I decided to do a little research on my own about this formulation. Reading about the formula was like digging into a good thriller novel. The original Protocel was called Entelev®. It was developed by a chemist named James Sheridan, a researcher at the Michigan Cancer Center. His research dates back to the 1930s. By controlling the energy needs of cancer cells, he theorized that he could selectively kill bad cells and preserve non-cancerous cells without damaging them. Sheridan eventually went to both the American Cancer Society and the FDA and never found approval. The National Cancer Institute did a study on Protocel and rejected it. The pro-Protocel group has a website describing the flaws in that NCI study. One website implies that the product is so powerful that the giant chemotherapy industry did not want to see it succeed. Whatever the case, they decided to use a grassroots approach instead. Protocel is now marketed on alternative cancer treatment sites and through nutriceutical specialists.

One woman spearheaded the effort to popularize Protocel. Author of the book *Outsmart Your Cancer*, Tanya Harter Pierce has a master's degree in psychology. When her family member got cancer, she started learning about alternative treatments, including Protocel. She compiled a number of impressive stories and testimonials about cancer survivors who used only Protocel as a salvage treatment and are still alive. The stories are uplifting, if not miraculous.

As a patient, I want to run out and buy Protocel immediately. If the data are even half true, it would be worth it. If it does nothing, the snake oil manufacturers will derive some income, and my loss would amount to a few bucks, some time and effort, and maybe an upset stomach. On the other hand, if the product works as well as the site suggests, then there really might be a panacea out there. Why not try it? There are a few issues with the product. It costs between $75.00 and $100.00 per month. It must be taken every four hours exactly, and some people say it tastes terrible. It has so many interactions that the list of other supplements to be avoided includes almost every other pill most of us take.

As a physician/scientist, I am trained to look for proof. We know that data can be manipulated to prove a point. There are no real, randomized, controlled, double-blinded studies proving the efficacy of Protocel. If the product is that good, I would expect some large company to underwrite the cost of proving it. I suspect that its contents, a mixture of proprietary antioxidants, are not considered a good enough bet to spend the money on to study. Antioxidants have started to fall out of favor with many medical researchers. Apparently, they are not proving to be as successful as they were thought to be. I refer you to the Internet to read up on the role of scavenging free radicals (how antioxidants work) in the prevention and treatment of cancer.

Reading about Protocel convinced me that it is nearly impossible to know where medicine ends and miracles start. I believe in both. If not Protocel, then noni juice or chelation. The list of alternatives is endless. Who knows? Those ads may one day be hanging in my playroom, and my children will be joking with me about the days when we all thought it was snake oil.

✳ ✳ ✳

SURVIVING LIFE

Low-Dose Naltrexone and Cancer

Again, I am thrilled to report that a reader introduced me to a novel cancer treatment I'd never heard of. It is called low-dose naltrexone (or LDN, for short).

In 1984, the FDA approved the drug naltrexone. It is a drug that blocks receptors for opiod narcotics—whether produced inside the body (internal) or given from an outside source (external). What is an opiod narcotic, you ask? Opiods narcotics are the active ingredient in codeine, morphine, hydrocodone, oxycodone, and heroin. Those are external opiod drugs. They are known to attach to receptors in your brain that result in the "high" feeling that makes them excellent for pain management. The patient on opiods might still be able to feel the pain, but it does not bother them as much. Internal opiods are produced in our bodies (in the pituitary and adrenal glands, for example), and we call them endorphins and metenkephalins. Their production is increased by various stimuli like exercise, which is why that great feeling you get after a run or workout is called a "high."

Naltrexone was introduced as an antidote for someone who is accidentally given or takes too much of an opiod. A good example is in obstetrics. If the mother is given narcotic pain medication during labor and the baby is born a bit sleepy, a tiny amount of naltrexone is given to reverse the effects of narcotics transferred through the umbilical cord. Likewise, street addicts found comatose are given the drug to "awaken" them from an overdose.

So how does a drug that interferes with opiods affect cancer? A psychiatrist in New York, Dr. Bernard Behari, determined that our immune system is sensitive to our internal (technically known as endogenous) opiods. During our normal sleep-wake cycle, there are periods when our endogenous opiods—the endorphins and metenkephalins—are at higher levels. He found that by giving patients tiny doses of Naltrexone, he "fooled" the brain into thinking that there was not enough opiods available, which led to increased endogenous opiod production. By "up-regulating" the system, especially between 2 a.m. and 4 a.m., he was able to get the immune system work better.

At first, Dr. Behari worked with HIV patients because they are known to have a loss of their immune function. Later, he transferred his study to the cancer arena. His work was pioneering. Now, there is complete acceptance of the role that the immune system plays in identifying and killing cancer cells. It is associated with an increase in the "natural killer" cell population, which is a powerful branch of our immune system that may not work right in some cancer patients.

LDN works in other ways, too. The endorphins it induces act directly on certain tumor cells leading to a spontaneous "apoptosis," or early cell death. The metenkephalins it induces attach to opiod receptors on tumor cells and causes an "anti-growth" phenomenon.

There are many websites devoted to LDN with links to the science behind it. I suggest www.LDNinfo.org. By no means is LDN designed to be a one-drug-fits-all panacea. But it may be valuable in the oncologist's armamentarium to use either in conjunction with other drugs or when most others have failed.

* * *

No matter what type of surgery, chemotherapy, radiation, mushrooms, or green tea, there is always personal and family fallout, as I call it. If you are aware of it and prepare for it, then you will be able to deal with what comes next.

7

During Treatment

You will not grow if you sit in a beautiful flower garden,
but you will grow if you are sick, if you are in pain,
if you experience losses, and if you do not put your
head in the sand, but take the pain and learn to
accept it, not as a curse or a punishment, but as
a gift to you with a very, very specific purpose.
—Elisabeth Kübler-Ross

Cancer changes everything from your self-identity to your interactions with family and friends. From diagnosis through survivorship, you must establish a "new normal" in your interpersonal relationships and with yourself.

The moment people found out I had cancer, they looked at me differently and talked to me differently. I now know that these encounters happen to practically all cancer patients. Common conversations become stilted, and social situations often are uncomfortable. Take, for example, the way people greet you. I was no longer Melanie, but Melanie with cancer; not Dr. Bone, but Dr. Bone with cancer. Maybe my closest friends acted normally, but more than one acquaintance averted their eyes when passing me, afraid to look right at me or speak to me. My professional colleagues, especially those who read my chart on the sly and saw for themselves the seriousness of my disease, acted like I was terminally ill. Believe it or not, children acted the most normal. Why? Because they have little or no experience with cancer. They see you for who you are, not how you look. If only everybody could see cancer patients through the eyes of a child, it might be easier to get through.

Perhaps because of the many uneasy social situations in which I found myself, I tended to shy away from outings during my treatments. This reclusiveness was highly unusual for me, a social butterfly. Cancer robbed me of the energy to get dressed up and put on a wig and a smile. I didn't feel like having women look across the room at me with sad eyes, thinking I didn't see them. I felt a little guilty for turning down so many invitations, but I realized that it was easier all the way around.

In December 2000, I was smack dab in the middle of my chemotherapy. Bald, anemic, weak, and with impaired immunity, I was in no shape to deal with the holidays. My brother and sister-in-law invited the six of us to fly up to Delaware for Christmas. My oncologist suggested that such a trip was risky for me. I'd just been to Las Vegas with my parents for a getaway, and wearing a mask on the airplane was a memory I'd like to erase. Ultimately, I decided to send the kids with my then-husband while I rested at home. Was I sad not to be with them when they were appreciating snow for the first time? Sure. But I felt some relief. I could get up late, take a bath, and eat Campbell's® chicken soup with stars and not have to share it. My advice to cancer patients: participate in what gives you pleasure, but don't be afraid to say no. With a little luck, there will be more celebrations in the future. Put yourself first, even if you are suffering mother-guilt. Now, many holiday seasons later, the children barely remember that I wasn't part of the experience.

Cancer patients anticipate feeling lousy during therapy. Chemotherapy gets such a bad rap that I can hardly believe I didn't throw up even once. My appetite was way down, mostly because I could not taste anything. Chemotherapy destroyed my taste buds. I would joke at the table, asking my daughter to pass the green cardboard (vegetables) or the brown cardboard (meat). As hard as it was for me to deal with this issue, it was harder for other people watching me not eat.

Family members see weight loss as a sign of illness. They associate an increase in appetite with being cured. My best advice is not to push the patient to eat. Have a variety of small, highly nutritious foods available. Sometimes, I could only get down a teaspoon of peanut butter or a bite of homemade macaroni and cheese casserole. My housekeeper left trail mix in a small bowl next to my bed and a bag of Hershey's kisses next to the couch. Smoothies or milkshakes with protein powder sometimes went down easier than solid food. When I was sick, there weren't many cancer cookbooks, but now there are a lot of guides to help nourish patients appropriately. Eventually, taste and appetite return with better health, and many a skinny cancer patient becomes a pudgy survivor who needs to go on a diet.

I found my inability to do endurance sports the most depressing part of cancer. Even the most athletic cancer patients may not be able to keep it up during their illness. Take Lance Armstrong. He is such an amazing role model because of his comeback. During my bad days, I would read his book and know that I would be back to sports eventually. I know some patients feel up to working out during treatment, but their family discourages it. Unless the oncologist advises against exercise, and I doubt they will, let the patient do what feels right.

Along with surgery, chemotherapy, and radiation, I was offered therapy. Every week or two, I would meet with a psychologist specializing in cancer patients. She helped me learn visualization techniques and how to use meditation and affirmations to get through tough times. I was a failure at this. All I really wanted to do was feel good enough to go for a run. To this day, exercise is my meditation. I may not be able to run anymore because of damage to my neck from all my treatments, but tennis and biking do more for me than any mantra.

Food and exercise is one thing. Body image is another. Almost 100 percent of cancer patients experience adjustments to inevitable changes to their bodies. Hair loss during chemotherapy is the most well-known. No matter how well-prepared you are for it, the shock of seeing yourself bald for the first time is undeniable. My head is so small that every wig I tried on was too big and uncomfortable. A lovely gentlemen found me a tiny wig, which I did wear on occasion. I still remember attending a formal event at the Mar-a-Lago Club in Palm Beach. I was wearing the wig. An old friend who hadn't seen me in a long time and was unaware of my cancer actually told me that my haircut was the cutest she'd seen it in years. I no longer wear head scarves or hats. Just the feel on my head brings back memories. I knew my hair would grow back, and it did. Never as thick as before and with a permanent bald spot, but it reminds me that the cancer cells are never coming back either.

Other scars are there forever. Each time I towel off after a shower in front of the bathroom mirror, they are there. Going to a spa where I watch other women watch me trying not to look like they are watching me is no longer fun. I can't lie on my stomach comfortably for a massage no matter how many pillows they use or promise to get me comfortable. I gave up on anything but a chair massage. Buying a swimsuit is torture. They all have elastic or built in bras, and the pressure is unbearable after an hour. These complaints are silly, but real. Cancer patients learn to cope with them over time, but during treatments, they can pose quite a challenge. Nowadays, I tell myself that my inability to tolerate a bra has saved me a lot of money that I would have blown at Victoria's Secret to restore uplift to what would have been a pair of very saggy breasts.

Sex was a huge problem. It is one of the hardest issues facing cancer patients. Most cancer patients put sex at the bottom of their to-do list. Their spouses or partners without cancer have sex higher up on the list. The patient may or may not feel guilty about this. The whole situation is uncomfortable. For example, chemotherapy causes most women to go through temporary or permanent menopause. They develop dryness, and sex becomes painful without using special creams. Men may lose their erections as a result of their prostate surgery. Couples with excellent communication skills are able to work through this difficult time. Alternate pleasuring is possible. For many, cuddling and lots of hugs carry them through to better times. The last time I reviewed the statistic, virtually 100 percent of cancer patients—especially breast and prostate cancer patients—have sexual dysfunction. Of course, the fact that my marriage was doomed by the time I was diagnosed no doubt contributed to this problem. Now, happily remarried, using local hormone replacement, intimacy has regained its place in my life. My erogenous zones are different, but since most libido is found between the ears, there is always hope for survivors.

SURVIVING LIFE

✳ ✳ ✳

Cancer and the Meditation Misfit

When I was first diagnosed with cancer, I started reading volumes about alternative treatments. Not that I was going to skip my surgery, chemotherapy, and radiation, but I wanted to complement it.

I was told that guided imagery and meditation were excellent approaches. Someone gave me an inspirational CD to get started. I put on headphones, closed the drape, and put an aromatherapy pillow over my eyes to get in the right mood.

The woman's voice was soothing and liquid. She began with breathing exercises. A lot of these tapes or CDs start that way. I think it has to do with concentrating on something that will distract your mind and empty it of other thoughts. It works.

The narrator then guides you through a walk in the forest, a beach scene, a boat on a lake, or some other serene experience to calm and soothe you. In addition to distraction, these exercises are designed to recruit your own immune system to fight off cancer cells.

Some of these tapes actually have you visualize the cancer cells and destroy them. I remember one that encouraged you to chomp up the cancer cells, like the game Pac-Man.

I used my tapes faithfully during treatment, never really sure if I was doing them correctly. When I got better and went back to work, I stopped doing them. It amazed me how easy it was to get wrapped up in the stressors of everyday life after facing my own mortality. Human nature is to revert back to what we were like before cancer.

Since cancer, I got divorced, moved, and took in a new partner at work. Between my professional and personal life, the stress is overwhelming at times. Try as I might to incorporate imagery or meditation to help cope with these pressures, I fail miserably.

Before cancer, I was Type A, and that hasn't changed. Now, when I make a concerted effort to meditate, other thoughts intrude, and I find myself more anxious about the fact that I can't get into that mellow place that awaits me. Worse yet, I start to feel guilty that I am unable to utilize relaxation tapes. Instead, I hear a narrator in my mind telling me that I could be a better person if I were able to release the issues and meditate successfully.

Truth is, I am a very intense person, and I don't find trying to wipe my mind clean of the billion random thoughts that cross it fun or beneficial. That's probably why I am not even a good sleeper. I can't wait to get to the next day and experience it to the fullest.

Luckily, I think I am not alone. I took a survey of my friends. What an eye-opening experience. Many of them had tried yoga or meditation and found the same problem as I did. They also felt like failures. I think I figured out what separated the successful meditators from the unsuccessful ones: aerobic exercise.

The friends who were runners or bikers or engaged in a regular aerobic exercise routine found that the time spent exercising fulfills their need for peace and distraction. The ones who didn't enjoy athletics and had no physical release had an easier time finding their peaceful place with mental relaxation exercises.

I feel so much better knowing that other "relaxation" failures are out there. And I still feel that my immune system is stimulated by exercise and is working as hard as ever to keep any rogue cancer cells at bay.

So for those of you meditation instructors pushing us hyper-survivors to learn to "slow down and relax," please give us a break. When our knees and backs give out, we might just join you.

SURVIVING LIFE

✳ ✳ ✳

Cancer Scars

I've never been a hard-bodied beauty, even at my most fit. I could train for a marathon for months and still boast cellulite and jiggly inner thighs. But, I knew I'd done my best and would proudly march through a locker room with the best of them on the way to the shower or hot tub.

Then came cancer.

I went into the operating room with two breasts, and I came out eight hours later with two pubertal mounds and no nipples. Over the course of the next year, I had them filled with saline until they became more the typical ice cream scoop shape, still with no nipples. I was one of the few lucky ones whose tissue expanders were their implants. At the end of my treatments, the plastic surgeon made a nick in my skin and pulled out the tubing that served as a filling conduit and, voila, I was finished—except that I had no nipples or areolae.

In clothes, this was no big deal. But naked, it was weird. I lost my innocence, and, like Eve in the Garden of Eden, I no longer felt comfortable wandering naked. And, while I had traded in a saggy set of 32A-Bs for a perky, firm set of 36B-Cs, the thought of going braless lost all its appeal. Actually, I used to dream of having a boob job so that I could wear more styles. Funny, after the mastectomies, I could care less that I don't need a bra and dread the day, if I make it to my 70s or 80s, how my wrinkled up corpse will look with teenage breasts.

It took quite a while for me to regain enough strength to try the gym. I had always used a personal trainer, so showering and changing in her bathroom was no different than at home. I ended up at a different gym and found myself unable to undress and take a shower there. I was embarrassed for me and for the other women there who I was sure would be staring at me on the sly, trying to glimpse what a cancer patient's breasts look like.

Then, a patient gave me a full day at a local spa for delivering her baby. I know she felt that it was an ideal gift for the frazzled, overworked ob-gyn in need of rest and recuperation. I have never used the gift certificate. I am too uncomfortable. I can't go into a public or even semi-private hot tub. My scars are right there for the world to see. Once I tried and could feel the tension in the spa. The other women wanted to look, but didn't want to look. I felt obligated to break the silence and ended up with a typical question-and-answer session about breast cancer. While I never have minded teaching others, I hadn't intended spa outings to be continuing medical education.

And what about the nipple issue? To get them, or not to get them? That is a big decision among breast-cancer survivors. From where to get them? Tissue grafts from the ear, the labia? Or plastic reconstruction using skin from the edges of the mastectomy scars? Tattoo areolae or not?

A year after my first surgery and months after finishing my chemo and radiation treatments, I opted for the nipple reconstruction. I found that looking at my breasts each day when I got out of the shower was enough of a reason to reconstruct. Here's the catch: I never particularly liked my nipples. They had started to point in the wrong direction after my fourth child. However, even I, the doctor, didn't understand that once you get them reconstructed, they are erect forever. Not a big deal if you can wear a bra. But for those of us whose surgery and radiation has rendered their chest and back so sensitive that they can't tolerate the pressure of a bra, the nipple erections can be painful. Breast petals or daily Band-Aid® application are a part of my routine. Who ever would have guessed?

After the Madonna-cone dressings came off my nipples, I began to cry. Not only did they look big, but they had no color. Enter the tattoo lady. I was so fortunate. A friend who is a nurse and a beauty treatment expert had a lot of experience in nipple/areola tattooing. She explained that it shouldn't hurt because of the numbness of the breasts after the surgery. Wrong! While I had no pleasurable sensations in the breasts, when the needle penetrated, I realized that I did have pain receptors deeper in the tissue. After some local anesthesia, we proceeded easily. She mixed red and blue and other pigments, and I left feeling so proud of my new, normal breasts.

I forgot that radiated tissue sometimes doesn't heal as well as non-radiated tissue. I ended up getting an infection and sloughing a portion of the tattoo. I still haven't gotten up the guts to try again—and the asymmetry of my nipples is yet another reason why I am not able to feel comfortable unclothed.

All in all, I've had a fairly easy go of it. I have talked to many women who have been traumatized by their reconstruction. TRAM flap failures, expander explosions, leaks, encapsulations, pain syndromes, and many more things happen to some patients. But what choice do we have? All of these are nothing compared with what would happen without treatment.

And in the long run, when I walk into a room fully dressed, with a smile on my face, I am the survivor I want to be: a happy inspiration to others.

SURVIVING LIFE

* * *

Cancer and the Senses

Of all the things I mourn after being treated for cancer, I miss not having the keen senses I did before chemotherapy.

It isn't all bad. Before cancer, I could smell a dirty diaper on someone else's baby at the other end of the room, and now I can't. When I am forced to sit next to a person with bad body odor, I can barely tell. Unfortunately, I also used to use my excellent sense of smell to help diagnose various infections and patient problems, and now I need to rely on other methods of detecting something that was obvious to me before I left the examining room.

Hand in hand with the loss of smell came a complete change in my taste buds. I used to yearn for the sweet aftertaste of a melted Hershey's kiss on my tongue because it would last far longer the candy itself. Now, I can taste the chocolate, but it is definitely not the same. Again, there are benefits. I used to struggle with maintaining my weight at 110. Now I am 95 to 100 pounds without trying. Food is not as exciting as it used to be without the smell/taste interaction.

As for touch, that too has been altered. Being numb from shoulders to the bottom of my ribcage has certainly changed my sexual experiences. Add to that the loss of feeling that comes with estrogen depletion at menopause (again brought on by the chemo and surgery to remove at-risk ovaries), and I am very much aware of the challenges of postmenopausal intimacy.

For those cancer survivors whose chemotherapy has left them with loss of sensation in the feet and hands/fingers, or worse yet, a constant painful tingling sensation in the extremities called neuropathy, just getting out of bed and stepping on the floor can be a nightmare, let alone trying to engage in normal, daily activities. I have a friend who was a fairly prolific writer. After her treatments, she had to give up trying to hold a pencil, so she tried typing. No good, as she can't handle a keyboard. She has taken to dictating and transcription, but says that her creative juices aren't flowing nearly as well without the use of her hands.

Visual changes related to cancer depend on the type. They are not uniformly a part of all patient experiences. The same goes for hearing. Should the cancer involve either the eye or the ear or the portion of the brain related to these senses, then these senses will be greatly affected. I find that most patients complain that they experience a premature aging of the senses. They need reading glasses earlier and find they can't listen to more than one conversation at the same time the way they used to. Whether this is a result of the treatment itself or the perception that once you have cancer you are "aged" in some way, is hard to tease out.

Fortunately, the human body has a great way of adapting to these issues. I remember hearing as a young girl that a blind person has a very acute sense of hearing and that deaf-mutes can feel vibrations of speech and music. The same goes for cancer patients that have a sense deficit. While I may not be able to tell if my child has soiled their pants, I can look for other clues that they need to be cleaned up; my replacement is fingernail inspection. If they have grimy nails, into the bath they go. If I can't taste the chocolate mousse the way I remembered, I try to imagine the taste and feel lucky that a spoonful or two satisfies me in a way that it never did.

One sense, generally not acknowledged as a sense, that I find is far sharper since my cancer, is the ability to empathize. I know how all those fears, aches, pains, and losses feel having been through them myself. I actually feel fortunate for that trade-off. I'd rather be a sensitive, caring person than be able to detect foul smells any day. And there is a keen sense of being able to remember when I had all those senses intact. Until I become senile, I can simply reach back into my memory and experience the senses I want.

Having brought up memory, I will say that my short-term memory is completely shot. But I have found ways around it. As a doctor, I enter my notes about patients on the day they are seen. No more procrastination because I won't remember their exam if I don't. The same goes with other day-to-day tasks. I keep a PDA with me at all times to jot down my to-do list so I won't forget. And the beauty of short-term memory loss is that long-term memory can come back into focus. Like my own parents, I find myself able to have a better recollection of earlier happenings in my life than I did when my short-term memory was better. See, for every black cloud, there is a silver lining.

People often marvel at my positive, optimistic attitude regarding cancer. If more cancer patients could stop looking at their disease as a war and stop considering themselves a victim, then we would be open to the opportunities that cancer has brought to us and live fully until our last day. Whether you have metastatic disease and a prognosis that is grim or have been cured, you are a survivor, and each day can be made better by letting the positives of survivorship enter your life. I often remind my patients who are anxious and neurotic about their health that they cannot control everything. They can be in "perfect" health and still be hit by a car while crossing the street or be stricken with cancer out of the blue. If they can just spend the effort they do on living rather than avoiding getting sick, then no matter how long their life, they would have been making the most and enjoying it.

SURVIVING LIFE

✳ ✳ ✳

Sex

Here is a telling statistic: 100 percent of breast-cancer survivors experience some form of sexual dysfunction. My guess is that it is the same for prostate-cancer survivors. Maybe it has to do with the fact that these cancers involve sexual organs, but then again, maybe not. It wouldn't surprise me if most survivors notice changes in their sex lives. Far be it from me to pretend to be the Masters and Johnson of survivors. But, as a survivor, I have some firsthand experiences, and, as a gynecologist, I have quite a bit of secondhand information to guide me.

Let's start with the obvious: the physical manifestations of cancer and their impact on a survivor's sex life. My comments may focus on breast cancer, but really can be applied to other cancers as well. When surgery, radiation, and/or chemotherapy are a part of the treatment, physical scars remain as a daily reminder. Lumpectomy or mastectomy both result in the loss of what was once a source of pleasure for most women. With each sexual touch thereafter is a constant reminder of cancer. After treatments, few patients report that they have sexual pleasure from foreplay involving their breasts, even if they have one intact breast. At worst, there is pain. Most commonly, there is numbness. Even I, a physician, never realized that my chest would no longer feel pleasure sensations after my mastectomies. What I am able feel is pressure, and if the pressure is too hard, then there is shooting pain, and there is not much erotic about the sensation.

Many spouses of breast-cancer survivors think they are being sensitive when they announce that their lovers' reconstructed breasts are still a source of sexual pleasure. But they don't realize that this comment is a double-edged sword. The patient wants to please her mate or feels a pressure to resume normal sexual function to prove the cancer is over. She doesn't want to say, "Please, don't touch my breasts even if they turn you on because each touch is a reminder of my cancer, and I can't feel anything anyway." Instead, she permits touching, which can result in resentment toward a partner who really had good intentions. He believes he will make her feel better by telling her she is still sexy to him. He can't fully empathize with her discomfort and may not be able to understand the delicacy of the whole issue. They say that the road to hell is paved with good intentions, and this is an example.

Many couples start to bypass the breasts altogether. For some, this works out just fine. I counsel that wearing lingerie or some type of cover-up helps. The negligee can allow looking without touching, creating a visual erogenous zone. If the couple can be creative, they find other sources of arousal, concentrating the other four senses (taste, smell, sight, and vision). If they don't adapt, sex changes radically—little foreplay and not enough time for the woman to become excited enough to climax. Many patients tell me that sex becomes a chore. They are happy to have it be over quickly because they no longer enjoy it.

If this is the case for breast cancer, what about other kinds of cancer? While I have personal experience with the physical challenges posed by breast cancer, I have learned about other sexual problems from patients with other kinds of cancer. Some gynecologic cancer surgery renders women incapable of intercourse altogether. Few of these women recover sexually. Their embarrassment, pain, and frustration often make even an attempt at having sex not worthwhile. Many patients get depressed. The medications we give them to treat depression often worsen the problem by decreasing their libido and making orgasm virtually impossible.

A lot of women go through menopause as a result of their treatments. The lack of hormones diminishes their libido, and vaginal dryness can make sex excruciating. Luckily, if they have a sensitive gynecologist, the dryness can be reversed. The libido is another story. Libido is 90 percent between the ears. It fluctuates throughout life. Few postmenopausal women have a high libido—no matter what Suzanne Somers says. I try to teach my patients that the less they have sex, the less they want it, and the less they want it, the less they have it. Kind of like going to the gym: once there, most are happy they went. And the converse is true: the more they do, the more they want to do, and so on. Just getting started is the hard part. If I can help eliminate the physical pain of intercourse, then they are far more likely to try.

I can only imagine what it is like for men, but my instincts tell me they have similar sexual obstacles as a result of cancer. Many prostate procedures render patients impotent or subject to erectile dysfunction or ejaculation difficulties.

Some wives have confided in me that their husband's cancer was the end of their love life. Without the ability to have intercourse, some men just stop trying to have any type of intimacy.

If sex after cancer becomes difficult or nonexistent, what impact does that have on the relationship? The answer is that it all depends on the relationship. Some weather storms well, and others do not. Some couples get very close and have the affection and caring of best friends. Others end with infidelity or divorce. Statistically it is about 50/50 that the marriage will survive. The 50 percent who do make it all share two important traits: patience and communication. Without them, you might as well move into another bedroom.

✳ ✳ ✳

From eating to sex, cancer patients encounter upheaval in their personal lives. Trying to accept both physical and emotional alterations is hard. Slowly, life starts to revert after treatments are done, but very few cancer patients feel their disease has gone without a trace. Before addressing survival, cancer patients must deal with what comes next: the family aftermath of this disease.

8

Family Fallout

Be who you are and say what you feel, because those who mind don't matter and those who matter don't mind.
—Dr. Seuss

During treatment, the patient suffers for sure, but there is always "collateral damage" to the family. They are afraid—afraid that their loved one may not get better or may never be the same even if they survive. They understand that family life has been turned upside-down. Over time, the "new normal" insinuates itself, and eventually the "old normal" becomes a memory. Luckily, there are no set rules of behavior, and each family has to make them up as they go.

What about the kids? If you think it is possible to keep cancer a secret from them, I would tell you to rethink that idea. Children are perceptive. They will see a change in their parent and will know something is wrong even if they aren't told. I know a woman who tried to keep her cancer a secret. She would get up super early to put on her wig. At home, she was able to keep up this act. She never dreamed her children would find out about her illness on the playground. While they were on the jungle gym, another child blurted it out. The children defiantly denied that anything was wrong, but the other child insisted that his own mother told him their mother was sick. When these children confronted their mother, it was a disaster. She was forced to admit she was sick and had lied to them. This damaged their trust. It took a lot of time and therapy to reestablish it. So, no matter how well-intentioned a parent's thought to protect a child from the truth, lying is a no-no. My best advice is to tell your children in a way they can comprehend. Remember, most children do not associate cancer with death, and for them, it is just a word. You have a rare opportunity to help rid the word of its bad reputation in the way you share the knowledge.

When my son Rex was two years old, the local newspaper interviewed him about my cancer. He told the reporter that the doctors had to cut off his mommy's boobies and throw them away because they were sick. He went on to explain that they put in water balloons and then pulled her hair out as part of the plan to get her better. To this day, Rex and I laugh about it. The lesson has stuck with me. Explaining cancer to children at an age-appropriate level will help them deal with it. The younger, the better. Unlike adults, who are unable to drop their preconceived notion of cancer equaling death, children see cancer for what it is: another illness that may well be cured.

Guiding your children through cancer may seem tough, but they respond to a lot of love and keeping to a schedule as best possible. Spouses and extended family are different. They need more than reassurance and have personal baggage from their own life experiences that affects the way they handle the disease. Therapists, books, and support groups can help. Most cancer centers have a special therapist available to guide patients, couples, and other family members through this tough time. It shouldn't be a surprise that women are more amenable to therapy than men. Men may respond better to reading a book about the situation. Support groups get a bad rap sometimes, but they can be a great help. Also, some people meet at a group, but then branch out on their own to make their very own group. Sometimes, support may be found in unlikely places.

Communication is the key to holding the family together during cancer. Learning your loved one's cancer "language" will help them more than imposing your own cancer "language" on them. Some spouses need to ignore cancer or minimize it or deny it altogether. Others not only get involved in it, but indulge it and become rabid activists about it.

✳ ✳ ✳

Cancer and Motherhood

I was examining a patient when the cell phone in my pocket vibrated. "Excuse me, but it might be one of my children," I explained. The patient graciously encouraged me to answer it. Sure enough, it was my son complaining of a stomach ache and headache at school and asking to be picked up. My daughter had the flu a week before, so it seemed reasonable. But something about the whining tone and the litany of complaints made me suspicious. "Do you have any sports games after school today?" I asked. "Yeah. Lacrosse. But it doesn't matter if I miss it." A maternal alarm went off in my head. My son wasn't sick. He didn't want to play the game. Getting sick was the logical, 11-year-old way out of it.

After explaining to my son that I would have someone pick him up, I had a friend get him and bring him right to my office. Over a quick lunch of sushi, I ferreted out the problem. It had to do with my son's ability as a goalie. He was new at the sport and worried that he would let the team down.

"What happens if you don't play? Who will be goalie?" I asked. "Nobody. We'll forfeit," he answered glumly. Here was a great opportunity to teach a life lesson, I thought. "Son, you have a lot of power right here in your own hands. If you don't play, you lose the game for the team. But if you do play, you might lose, or you might win. At least you might have a good time playing. I am not going to force you to play, but I am going to ask you to think about your teammates and friends and decide what you want to do. The power and the decision are both yours."

He came to the conclusion on his own that it would be better to play, and he did. They lost the game, but he had a few great saves and came home bubbling over with excitement about it.

I am proud of that instance of parenting. Before cancer, it would have played out differently. First, I probably never would have even heard from my own child about the illness. The school would have contacted either my then-husband or my housekeeper, and one or the other would have gone over to get him. Instead of taking time out of my day to sit with my child to figure out the cause behind the stomach ache, I felt comfortable to have him in safe hands until I was finished at work and could get home to see him.

So how did cancer change my behavior as a parent? Easy. I came to realize that the zillions of hours I was spending working to take care of everyone else and their families was time away from my own family. You might think that knowing that is really basic, but remember, many physicians have caretaker personalities and can't help but be there for their patients and put everyone close to them last. After cancer, a light bulb went off in my head. I realized that if I don't get involved in my children's lives, then I am guilty of letting them be raised by "staff." Before cancer, I justified my minimal family involvement by believing that working hard made me a great role model. The time I eked out to spend with the children was quality time, and it didn't matter if I was there a lot; I just had to make the moments with them intense. My sister was a lawyer who stopped working to raise her children. She told me that she thought it was more about quantity than quality. I always thought that it was her excuse for not heading back to the world of law. While I no longer feel that way, I do have a different insight.

The middle road is where the happiness lies. I can't imagine myself, a lifelong professional, giving it up to be a full-time mom, but my cancer experiences taught me that I want to be there for a lot more of my children's school performances, lost lacrosse games, and triumphs and tragedies. At least, if my cancer ever returns, I will feel that I have given them the foundation to be whatever they choose: mother, professional, or some combination and the memories to take them there.

SURVIVING LIFE

✳ ✳ ✳

Family Aftermath

Entering the exam room, I noted from her chart that the patient in for her annual pelvic exam was a healthy 37-year-old. Sue is a chatty and upbeat mother of three and we'd shared funny stories about our children during prior visits as a distraction while I did the pap smear. I set the chart down and was rinsing my hands as I asked the usual, "How's it going? Anything new?" I turned around while drying my hands to find her eyes red and brimming with tears. Resetting my mood, I sat on the stool at the end of the exam table, waiting to start examining her until I figured out what was wrong. Over the next five minutes, she explained that her father just finished treatments for throat cancer. He was doing well and beginning to gain weight. Sue was most upset because everyone else was thrilled that he was doing well and yet she was not coming around.

"I feel like I've aged 10 years and I didn't even have the cancer! Look at me! I'm a mess." She pointed to her own very attractive face, but the stress had indeed taken its toll. There were no obvious wrinkles or sags. She just looked wiped out.

Thank goodness her exam was normal. We spent time discussing the problem. It was easier for me to understand her situation. Women tend to face cancer differently than men. For her father and brother, the cancer was a "problem" that was treated with surgery, chemotherapy, and radiation. Unless and until it came back, it would not be acknowledged again. This attitude may be denial, but it works for many. For Sue, the trauma of the cancer, memories of treatments, and fear of recurrence were as strong after the last chemotherapy as before they started. She remains in "caregiver limbo," as I refer to it.

During cancer, attention is focused on the patient, and deservedly so. Support groups are available for family and friends, but are underutilized. Caregivers' lives are disrupted as much as the patient's life. Leaving her children to escort her father to another city for treatment every few weeks was traumatic for Sue. No matter where she stayed nor how nice the staff, it wasn't home. She felt obligated to sit in a chair by his side, ruminating about laundry left at home, carpooling to soccer, and the fact that her husband, Dave, never shampooed the kids the way she does. She missed her regular yoga and tennis, key to her stress management. The children tortured her unintentionally by telling her they missed her. Worse yet, reporting all the "stuff" she missed felt like a knife to the heart. They are too young to understand that they may find themselves in the exact same situation one day…the woes of an adult child.

Sue's father, on the other hand, was retired when he got his cancer. Rearranging his schedule had less of an impact on his life. He was not struck in the prime of his life and he, a religious man, put his faith in a higher power to see him through. He discouraged his daughter from setting aside her life for him, but was grateful for her company. He worried more about her than himself.

Sue has a brother. He is less involved. He wants Sue to be content that their father has no cancer at the moment. He does not want to "ask" for trouble by playing the "what if" game that Sue does. His behavior allows him to move on with his daily life. I explained to Sue my personal theory that, as former hunter-gatherers, human males are hard-wired to compartmentalize their feelings. It allows them to continue providing for their families. If they let cancer-related fears paralyze them, they might fail to support their family.

So where does that leave Sue? The survival process is going to be just that for her, a process. She needs to experience it, not compartmentalize it. I suggested that she go back to her pre-cancer routine. She needs to talk to someone about her feelings. While she may worry that her father and brother are unrealistic about a recurrence, she would do better discussing it with a professional. I reassured her that her feelings are normal and gave her the name of a woman who specializes in cancer-related counseling.

I walked to the next exam room emotionally exhausted, but feeling better for helping. The joy of being a cancer-survivor-doctor. Thankfully, the next patient only needed a refill on her birth control….

❋ ❋ ❋

SURVIVING LIFE

What a Mother Will Do

Friday. After a long week, we faced an hour-long trip to Fort Lauderdale to my son's debate tournament. Eric and I were chaperones of the two-day event. By dinnertime, I was fading and the competition was still going strong. I decided to check into the hotel and Eric would follow later with the boys.

The Hampton Inn was already decorated for Halloween. Pumpkin candy dishes on the counter and black cat cutouts turned the lobby into a homey place. I stepped up to the check-in desk and the woman, Lilly (by her nametag), smiled and said, "Welcome Dr. Bone." I was shocked. How did she know my name? She told me that only a few guests were due in and she could just tell I was Dr. Bone. Women's intuition. Then I saw the ribbon on her lapel. Not the infamous pink. It was orange—a strange Halloween ribbon. She saw me looking and explained. "My daughter has cancer. Leukemia."

Even though I was tired, we connected. For me, sharing cancer experiences is invigorating. Her daughter's acute leukemia was diagnosed on an Easter morning when Sophia was 18 months old. This cancer is usually curable in young children, but Sophia's is still not completely under control two years later. The child spent months in the hospital when the port placed into her chest for chemotherapy became infected and nearly killed her. The wallet-sized picture Lilly showed me was of a chubby-cheeked cutie dressed in pink from head to toe. As a doctor, I could tell that her pudginess was from steroids, not from eating too many candy corns.

Lilly looked tired. Her job is a lifeline to health insurance so she has no choice but to leave Sophia for long stretches. There is nothing a mother won't due for a child she loves—whether it's missing her weekend plans to sit in a stuffy high school library for hours on end while her son competes in debate or working nights and weekends to make sure her daughter's cancer gets treated.

Is it worth it? When my son walked up on the stage and accepted a trophy as big as I've ever seen for placing first, I was on top of the world. When Lilly watches Sophia perform at her first dance recital or get her first diploma, she will certainly agree that, whatever it took, it was worth it.

❋ ❋ ❋

There is no one right approach to supporting each other through cancer, but with good treatment and some luck, survivorship comes next.

9

Early Survivorship

Every challenge can teach us something about ourselves—
to be open to this learning is the beginning of success.
—Inspired by American Indian philosophy

I still remember the last day of my treatments. It was a complete letdown. The radiation therapy facility was quiet, and I did not even wait five minutes before hearing the familiar voice on the speaker: "Dr. Bone to the back. Dr. Bone to the back." The locker room had a full-length mirror on the wall, and I looked at my bald head and powdered-on eyebrows. It didn't feel any different from the last 35 visits. The technician helped me into position, and the machine buzzed for about two minutes. I dressed and left. No special goodbyes. No parties. No well wishing. Once in my car, I looked into the rearview mirror and noticed that one of my eyebrows had rubbed off completely. I looked weird. I felt weirder.

Was that it? I'd been going to doctors' appointments and treatments and blood draws and scans every week for months. Now, I was supposed to resume my normal life until the first follow-up appointment in four weeks. I felt like I'd jumped out of an airplane and was free falling.

Most cancer survivors agree that the first one to five years of survivorship are really hard. There is constant anxiety that the cancer will come back. Somehow, when you are actively treating it with chemotherapy and radiation, you feel more comfortable than when you are told that it's time to stop and see what happens. In the very beginning it's hard to overcome the urge to schedule an emergency appointment with some medical caregiver for any ache or pain that comes up. For me, the wait for that first visit back to my oncologist, my lifeline, felt like an eternity. When she came into the room, cheerful and all smiles, it was hard not to jump on her with a million questions about possibilities.

Soon I returned to work, and my schedule looked more and more like it did before cancer. But now my life felt like a "lite" version of the old one. Instead of 40 to 50 patients a day, I could only see 10 to 20. I was slower to take a history, slower to examine a patient, and slower to write a note. My short-term memory was so bad that I had to write everything down not to forget it before I got to my desk.

I started to get more involved in my family instead of observing them from a chair on the side of the room. Soccer games, dance recitals, and parent-teacher conferences were put back on my schedule. A newfound need to spread awareness and educate about cancer resulted in additional commitments to speak at events, write a column, and become a "crusader."

Now, almost a decade since my diagnosis, I can honestly say that my cancer is not the first thing I wake up thinking about, nor is it the last thing I fall asleep thinking about. Does cancer enter my mind every day? For sure. But those thoughts no longer evoke as strong a reaction, and my feelings about cancer have mellowed considerably. That evolution happens slowly and without the cancer patient really being able to control it. Along the way, from frequent panicky thoughts about recurrence to the place where you are able to appreciate your cancer for all the good that it has done, there are a few stages that I believe most survivors pass through.

After the anxiety, there is often a time where survivors feel the need to give back to other cancer patients. They may opt to become a volunteer for a cancer group. Some people, me included, use their story to try to help others get through. The most outspoken become political advocates for cancer groups. Just about all of us raise money, walk in a cancer walk, or participate in some charitable activity related to our cancer. Eventually, some people move on and no longer have that need to be as involved with their cancer. Others remain lifelong participants in something related to their cancer. There is no right path to take. But remember, it does not mean that you are no longer grateful for your survival if you decide not to give money to a cancer cause one year or feel unmotivated to walk in a cancer walk.

SURVIVING LIFE

* * *

When Are We Cured?

The other day I received a call from a dear friend who had finished her cancer treatments a few months before. "I have amazing news," she bragged. "I am cured of my cancer. My oncologist just told me."

Alarms went off in my head. How can she be so naive? Nobody can declare a patient "cured" of cancer just three months out from treatment. The oncologist probably said that she had "no evidence of disease" ("NED" in the business). She interpreted that to mean she is cured. Doctors use a few different phrases to describe the situation when a patient is no longer receiving treatment, and shows no sign of cancer, but is not technically cured. The phrases NED and NDD (no demonstrable or detectable disease) are used interchangeably. They imply that the exam and scans do not find any cancer. The patient could have microscopic cancer and still be NED or NDD.

These phrases are interpreted differently by different patients. It is very similar to the cup that is either half empty or half full. Some patients find no solace in being NED. They want their doctor to take a stance and report that they are cancer-free, or better yet, cured. Others appreciate the honesty, understanding that being NED is the best they can ask for at the time.

In fact, the majority of the patients are cancer-free after their treatments. But mislabeling those who are destined to have a recurrence as cured is a big disservice. So we cater to the minority. Doctors leave wiggle room in their words.

If a patient recurs down the road, the oncologist can say without guilt that the patient was NED or NDD three months before, and had not been declared cured or cancer-free mistakenly.

So goes the quagmire of discussing cancer. Oncologists hedge their bets by using ambiguous words, and patients hear and interpret information individually. Semantics are key. Words have power. For some patients, hearing they are NED is the same as being cured. It is like unlocking the door to living again. These patients have been walking on eggshells, waiting to be told that they can move on. The news of remission—be it for a month, a year, or a lifetime—is enough for them.

Other patients who are told they are NED let their minds go to the implied uncertainty in the statement. They come right back at the doctor with pithy questions, zeroing in on the fact that the terms NED or NDD leave open the possibility that sub-clinical or undetectable disease may be present. Certain personality types cannot help but go down that darker path of fear. There isn't much any doctor can do to alleviate those fears, except suggest that the patient find counseling. Some patients need medication to treat the depression and anxiety that happens because they are fixated on the "what ifs" of recurrence.

My personal feeling is that NED or NDD is as good as cancer-free. Why? Because those same patients already went through a stage *before* they were diagnosed when they were NED and leading fairly normal lives. The cancer was there, but it didn't get in the way of living. Once patients are treated, many revert to that same situation. The difference is knowledge. I think of it as a little bit like Adam and Eve in the Garden of Eden. Once they partook of the forbidden fruit, their innocence was gone, and they began to see the world from a new perspective. Many cancer patients report that they were okay in the time before they were diagnosed. Even patients with extensive disease will tell you that they were doing fine up until someone diagnosed them as having cancer. A rare patient with terminal cancer tells me that they were virtually asymptomatic before they were told they had cancer. Symptoms didn't start until the treatments started. Taking patients back to the "place" they were prior to diagnosis, even if they harbor undetectable cancer, could feel a path back to innocence.

In some ways, all of us are NED or NDD. After all, 50 percent of the population is going to develop cancer. Almost every detectable cancer passes through a stage where it is not detectable. During that time, most people are living normal lives with NED. Then, they go on to the stage where the disease is detectable. And if we are not destined to get cancer, we are certain to face some life-threatening situation which will be comparable.

So, is there a time when anyone can really say with confidence that a cancer patient is cured? The old standard was to use the word "cured" after five years without any recurrence. Statistically speaking, about 95 percent of patients that make it to five years without a recurrence are "home free" as far as that cancer is concerned. A handful of cancers can come back many years later. Some patients, especially those who have a genetic predisposition to getting cancer, develop a new primary cancer. If it is the same organ, let's say breast cancer in the opposite breast, it may be confused with the old cancer "coming back." When the cancer involves a different organ, the pathologist can confirm that the tumor is new and not a metastasis (spread from the first cancer).

When I felt like jumping through the phone to shake my friend and remind her that she has at least four-and-a-half more years before she can feel "safe," I stopped. Who am I to burst her bubble? Even if she has a recurrence, she might as well feel good right up until that time. And if she never has a recurrence, who was I to put fear in her way?

SURVIVING LIFE

✳ ✳ ✳

Dreaded Scans

For years, I've suffered with an achy neck. It hasn't interfered with work or sports, but it chronically hurts.

An MRI done a long time ago showed that I had a "precocious" neck (as my doctor called it)—a cute description of the arthritic changes more often seen in a 70-year-old that started acting up after my cancer treatments finished when I was 40.

As long as I knew that the pain wasn't cancer, I could deal with it. Thank goodness for Advil® and those hot packs from the drugstore. Then, over the last year, I developed itching on my arm along with my neck ache.

A smart dermatologist figured out that an irritated nerve probably caused the rash on my arm from constant scratching.

My oncologist suggested another neck MRI, just to be sure. I stuffed the prescription in my purse to gather dust. My family, friends, and office staff, tired of watching me scratch, pressured me to get the scan.

As an eight-and-a-half-year cancer survivor, I all but ignore my anxiety about a recurrence—except when I am going for a scan. Then, I have two voices in my head. The doctor in me tells me how well I've done and focuses on the statistical chances (very low) that my longstanding neck pain and arm itching are due to cancer coming back. The patient in me is still terrified.

I rejected all offers for company to my scan appointment, deciding to face the day by myself. I figured that if the news was good, a cell-phone call would let everyone know. If my cancer had come back, I wanted some time alone to digest it before facing anyone, even those I love most.

Before the scan, I went to breakfast with a friend who is a retired oncologist. We reviewed the possible outcomes to help prepare me, and then moved to other, distracting topics. Soon, it was time to leave, and I drove the few blocks to the radiologist's office.

Luckily, I had an early appointment and did not have to wait at all. In a flash, I was in the machine. The scans were uneventful until I thought we were done. I popped up off the table to go get dressed.

The technician came in to tell me that the doctor wanted a few "extra" views of my neck. That pushed my fear button. I lay back down and closed my eyes for another 12 minutes in the magnet. My mind was racing. I went through every possible cancer-recurrence scenario. I chided myself for daring to be as optimistic as I'd been a few hours before at breakfast.

Memories of my diagnosis in 2000 intruded, no matter how hard I tried to force myself to be calm. I had begged and bartered with a higher power to let me live to see my children, then ages 2, 3, 4, and 5, finish elementary school.

Now, still in the MRI machine, I was asking for high school, imagining myself at my daughter's graduation, ravaged by the disease, bald, and confined to a wheelchair.

The technician brought me back to reality when he announced that the scan was over and led me to the dressing room before speaking with the radiologist.

I entered his office shaking. He turned around with a big smile and said, "Happy New Year. You don't have cancer." I started to cry. Out of gratitude. Out of embarrassment. Out of relief. Yes, my neck is the source of my symptoms, but they are all treatable.

I left his office feeling about 50 pounds lighter and used up my cell-phone battery calling everybody with the news. Then, I chastised myself for getting so worked up and vowed not to do it next time. But I know, as a survivor, I probably will.

SURVIVING LIFE

✳ ✳ ✳

Cancer and the Great "Turnaround"

People love a great "turnaround." What do I mean? We are suckers for a rags-to-riches or a bad-boy-turns-nice story. It may be that we are drawn to a great "turnaround" because it reminds us that we can reinvent ourselves. If we have traits that we are not proud of, embarrassing behaviors, or are just tired of our neuroses, we can dream about doing a great "turnaround," which will put us back on track to happiness and fulfillment.

Cancer is the perfect great "turnaround" opportunity.

I just got back from the Florida Obstetrics and Gynecology Society (FOGS) annual meeting in Naples, Florida. Not only was the hotel beautiful, but the meetings were intellectually stimulating, and the atmosphere was collegial. I can't recall the last time I'd attended a FOGS meeting. It was years ago. I had been active in the organization but resigned as a member of the executive committee when I was ill. I thought I would die before my turn at president and worried that I wouldn't have the stamina to do a good job representing over 1,000 obstetricians and gynecologists in Florida. Seeing old friends and new faces now that I have been in remission for a time was both great and emotional. It brought back a lot of bittersweet memories. Most of all, I felt reconnected. The attendees exchanged business cards and email addresses with plans to stay in touch.

The last night there was a dinner dance with a Motown band. Just as I was about to get up to dance, a balding gentleman came to sit beside me. He was familiar, but I had a hard time placing him. Not unusual for my chemo-brain and postmenopausal state. I glanced furtively at his nametag and saw he was from my own town of West Palm Beach. Then, it all came together, and I realized exactly who he was. In his day, he was considered an elegant surgeon and had a reputation as a no-nonsense doctor. These were good traits for a practicing gynecologic oncologist.

He took my hand in his and looked at me with misty eyes. "I read your column every week," he said. "It really helps me." He then went on to tell me that last fall he was diagnosed with stage IV lung cancer. He went to one of the meccas of cancer medicine, and they told him to forgo treatment. They even suggested that he begin hospice care. He did not want to give up. He ended up treating with a local oncologist with whom he has an excellent rapport. Miraculously, his cancer responded. He was happy to report that his last PET scan was negative.

He spoke with gratitude and humility. Peace and inner contentment emanated from him. This demeanor was a far cry from the high-powered physician whom I had heard about in the past from mutual colleagues. It seems that cancer brought about a great "turnaround" in him.

We chatted for a while, swapping war stories about chemotherapy. We'd both lost our hair and our fingernails, but found an inner spirituality that we hadn't connected with before. It was especially sweet, sharing that feeling we'd had when others had written us off, and surviving in spite of them.

I started thinking what a privilege it was to have experienced the great "turnaround." Not long ago, a friend invited me to attend an Adult Children of Alcoholics meeting. With no alcoholism in my family, I wasn't sure I belonged, but welcomed a new experience. The room was full of people who had been through traumas as awful as cancer. Many seemed to have also done a great "turnaround."

So it need not be cancer. It need not be alcoholism or any specific reason for the great "turnaround." It does require finding spirituality. Not necessarily Christianity, Judaism, Islam, or any other recognized named religion. For the doctor I spoke with, I believe it was a general spiritual awakening. For me, it was and still is the spirituality of helping others.

I felt a rush of warmth and good feeling when I stepped onto that dance floor, knowing that my column helped a retired doctor find his great "turnaround"— and it was all made possible by cancer.

✳ ✳ ✳

Around the five-year mark is a transition from an "early" survivor to a "long-term" survivor. For certain cancers, making it to five years is the same as saying you are cured. For others, such as melanoma, there is never really a time to say the patient has a definite cure. Long-term survivorship comes next.

10

Late Survivorship

What does not destroy me, makes me strong.
—Friedrich Nietzsche

What happens when a cancer patient is 10 years out from their diagnosis? Is that person still identified as a survivor? Of course. They are always survivors. Many survivors choose to put their cancer diagnosis well behind them—up in the attic, so to speak. Will they always have a tender spot in their brain that flares up when a cancer reminder ignites the flame? Definitely. For the most part, however, these patients are back to a normal life. Some people become defined by their survivor status, and it continues to be the driving force in their life. Many successful cancer organizations are run by long-term survivors. I don't believe a person intentionally decides to carry their survivor status like a lifelong backpack. It is a part of their basic personality. Why do you think I am writing this book? I am no different than many survivors who wish they could put cancer in the attic, but cannot. Therapy and distraction help. An intervening illness such as high blood pressure or osteoporosis can be a useful way to refocus their attention away from cancer. Any significant life event can do the same.

Another trait I notice is what I call "survivor burnout." The first few years after my diagnosis, I *had* to run the Race for the Cure®. I felt proud when the Komen Foundation asked me to ride in the pace car. Each time an opportunity presented itself to speak about cancer, I happily accepted. Then, I hit a wall. I didn't want to do it anymore. At the same time, I felt guilty that I wasn't as interested in "the cause" as I had been earlier on. Now, I realize my feelings are normal. An oncologist who I am now proud to call a close friend, Dr. Stan, sat with me over coffee one day to talk about this very problem. Letting go of a label that has done so much for you is really hard. He wisely explained that I should not see it as "letting go" of my cancer, but rather allowing my cancer identity to have the same power as my "doctor" identity or my "mother" identity or my "wife" identity. This approach made more sense than other people's explanations of how to resolve the conflict. It feels good to keep my cancer close, but no closer than it needs to be. When I do things like write this book, I am picking and choosing how I relate to cancer, not letting cancer control me.

A trip to the Canadian Rockies with my then-fiancé, Eric, proved to me that I was following Dr. Stan's advice. Then, a women's trip to the Turks and Caicos reinforced the importance of friendship in maintaining a stable, long-term survivorship. Going to New York City 17 years after I ran the New York Marathon reminded me of the enormous changes my life that had taken in the intervening years, cancer making it all the better. Now, I am at the point where I need to make New Year's resolutions again, instead of praying to live another year.

✳ ✳ ✳

Cancer and Charity

On a recent family outing, we stopped the van at a busy intersection in West Palm Beach. The man who approached our car looked dirty and disheveled. He did not appear psychotic. He carried a sign made of black marker on brown cardboard. It read: "Out of work. Have cancer. No home. Need help." All of us in the car felt very uncomfortable. It is common to see a homeless person on the corner asking for money with a sign. It is the perfect opportunity to teach my children a life lesson. I "lecture" about the importance of learning a skill or a profession and handling money responsibly to avoid finding themselves on the street, panhandling. The difference with this man was the line "Have cancer." My children know I am sensitive about people suffering, but even more so about people suffering from cancer. In this case, I also felt that this man was manipulative. He was using his cancer diagnosis to elicit sympathy from me and other drivers. Not that I didn't believe him, but how was I to be sure that he really had cancer? Just as I was deciding whether to give him money, the light turned green. We drove on, leaving the man to ask the cars at the next red light.

I looked at my children in the rearview mirror and asked them what they felt about the situation. They all felt that the man might be scamming them. While they all want to do something charitable for cancer patients, especially ones with whom they are friendly, they explained that giving money to the man on the street corner did not constitute their preferred form of charitable giving. I completely agreed with them. Our family has done a variety of charitable gestures, and we seem to like to give quality time, food, transportation, and companionship.

The encounter with the homeless man left me thinking about cancer and charity. Almost every type of cancer has at least one (if not many) charitable organization associated with it. Take breast cancer. There are so many breast cancer charities that it became necessary to create an umbrella organization to link the various charities. Some of the organizations are devoted to increasing awareness about breast cancer, some concentrate on raising money for research, some use the money they raise to help cancer patients pay for their care. Some cancer charities pay for special experiences for patients nearing the end of their life. Others help families of cancer patients pick up the pieces after their loved one dies. Some charities are devoted to cancer prevention. Some are looking for links between cancer and the environment. Each of these charities is trying to raise money to do their chosen mission. Even for those "in the know," it is hard to figure out which charity deserves our hard-earned dollars. Is there a way to figure out where and how much you should give?

Sometimes the charity finds you. Every day, Americans throw out envelopes from charitable organizations asking for money. If someone close to them is affected by cancer, they may chose to open one of the envelopes and donate. Sometimes, the envelope entices the recipient to give because it includes free address stickers or a colored ribbon to put on your car. These freebies are a form of thanks given in exchange for a donation. Give once, and you are guaranteed to receive more and more solicitations because most charities have computer systems that track this data.

Some people donate because they are interested in a specific aspect of the cancer and find a charity or an institution working on that aspect of cancer. For example, I have a friend with cancer who is now inspired to reduce chemicals and additives in her foods. She now eats organically and values "natural" treatments for cancer. She is inclined to give to charities that are involved in developing alternative cancer therapies. Another example is a patient who finds out their family carries a genetic predisposition to cancer, and so that patient donates to charities or educational institutions that research genetics and cancer.

Unfortunately, some of us are so overwhelmed by the number and variety of cancer charities that we can't decide. Instead, frozen by a fear that we may be wasting our money or donating it to the wrong charity, we just do not donate at all.

One common concern is that the donation will not be used on the mission of the organization, but on supporting the infrastructure of the charity. The most well-known charities have large public relations budgets. Some spend a lot of money prevailing upon celebrities to represent them. Many Americans are very interested in hearing about a celebrity with cancer. Having a famous person representing the cancer cause increases the likelihood that people will donate. While it may be off-putting to donate to an organization that uses a good portion of their budget on public relations, it is exactly that advertisement that brings the charity to the forefront of people's minds. Charities that do not advertise may not be found by donors and so not be able to get any charitable work done.

So what is the best way to find the best fit for you and a cancer charity? Certainly, it might be worth your while to log onto the charity's website to make inquiries about the organization. They are required to publish statistics that are important. They must report how much of each dollar donated goes to overhead, such as the salary and benefits of the executive director. They also must demonstrate that they are accomplishing their mission. All of these data are available for those prospective donors willing to find them.

Personally, I like to give in ways that I can see I am making a difference. For example, one of my favorite charities is one that does mobile mammograms for indigent and underserved women. The executive director of this organization, called the H.O.P.E. Project, is the same person who performs the mammograms. The radiologists who read the mammograms either donate their time or are reimbursed at a discounted rate. It has one mammography vehicle and operates in Palm Beach County. To my mind, giving locally to a smaller charity makes me feel like I am giving back to my own community. While I also try to give to larger, national organizations, I feel most satisfied when giving close to home. Other donors, especially those who have specific talents, are able to give "in kind." When the H.O.P.E. van needs repairs, a local shop can do them. If the van needs painting or new upholstery, there is a chance that a nearby small business owner will donate their services. They can then proudly announce that they gave of their time and resources. The opportunities are vast.

Now, back to my children and the man on the street. My children have been encouraged to be charitable from the time they were old enough to understand that they could help others. We have an agreement. They take part of their allowance and put it in the bank for college. Part of it goes to buying themselves a treat. A portion goes into a change jar. It is our charity money. After we have saved a jarful, we pick where we want to give it. We have purchased gifts for cancer patients. Once, we brought a cancer patient dinner. This type of giving is heartfelt and homegrown. I will never forget what I was taught as a child: the best gift is to give to others. Pay it forward.

✳ ✳ ✳

SURVIVING LIFE

The Power of Friends

A few weeks ago, one of my friends invited me on the first annual Amazing Women's Trip. My hostess planned this trip as a tribute to the three women she feels are her most important role models: a doctor, a lawyer, and a real-estate professional. Her goal was for us to meet each other. She predicted we would get along. She was absolutely right. From the moment we stepped onto the plane until the final misty goodbyes, the conversation flowed as freely as the rum punch. We were strangers on Sunday morning and best friends forever on Tuesday evening.

Two of us were cancer survivors, and the third had survived other traumas that might as well have been cancer. We were all more than 15 years older than our hostess, but for those few days we felt like high-school students, and the age difference was immaterial. After swimming, spa treatments, and sleeping under beach umbrellas, we decided to go snorkeling. I was excited to go, but

I am plagued by a fear of the ocean. I didn't want to spoil the trip, so I chose not say anything ahead of time, telling myself that all I had to do to overcome my fear was jump in and go ahead with a good attitude. After all, I've been told a million times that attitude is everything. We anchored by a spectacular reef, and I jumped in with masks and fins. About 100 yards from the boat, I felt the anxiety creep up my back. The fish were gorgeous, and with a friend's hand just a foot or two away, I was able to snorkel. Then, I looked down. Directly beneath me was a fairly large shark. I panicked. Within seconds, I was back on the boat, shaking with residual fear and embarrassment. The other three made their way back to the boat to see about the commotion. I felt ashamed and apologized for ruining their outing. We spent about half an hour talking it out, and they convinced me to try one more time. Captain Sean moved the boat to a conch farm in very shallow water, and I successfully picked one off the ocean floor. It may not seem like much of a feat, but I was proud that I did it, and my new friends cheered me on. All in all, the experience was special.

I got home and replayed that afternoon over and over again. It certainly was a learning experience. There is no doubt I was traumatized by a shipwreck that I was involved in at 12 years old. My whole family was stuck 50 miles offshore in the ocean, waiting to be saved. By the time the helicopters arrived 20 hours later to pick us up off the reef where our boat had crashed, the damage had already been done. Now, 35 years later, I still cannot enter the sea without having that gut-level fear overtake me—even in crystal clear water up to my knees.

In some ways, I have conquered my cancer fears more easily than my ocean fears. But every day, I meet women and men for whom cancer was a shipwreck that has remained traumatic forever. It can be hard for physicians who optimistically report that you have a 95 percent chance of being cured to understand that it isn't about the 95 percent. It is all about the 5 percent—the 5 percent that causes chronic anxiety and episodes of out-and-out panic.

The Amazing Women's Trip also reinforced what I know about friendship. These women gathered around to help me get back into the water in much the same way that my friends did when I was first diagnosed with cancer. In the four days I spent in the hospital recovering from surgery, my girlfriends painted and decorated my bedroom. They wanted me to be comfortable and cozy when I got home. During my chemotherapy treatments, they were a fabulous support group, listening to chronic complaints and doing the stuff of life that needed to be done to keep my family going during rough times. Without them, I am not sure I would have made it. For many people, family does all this. But for some of us whose families are so overwhelmed, friends are better helpers.

Without the Amazing Women's Trip, I am certain that I would have never even tried to do a snorkel adventure. More importantly, with the women on the Amazing Women's Trip, I would not be looking at the gorgeous conch shell that now sits on my mantle.

✳ ✳ ✳

New York Marathon: 17 Years Later

Sometimes, I worry that I can barely remember life before cancer. Many survivors call their lives after cancer the "new normal," which makes great sense. What amazes me is that my memories of pre-cancer events are colored by cancer.

A perfect example happened this weekend. Eric and I went to New York City for a quick getaway. The Big Apple still has signs up, advertising the New York Marathon, run a week ago. Seventeen years and one week ago, I was in New York to run the marathon. I finished in 4 hours 23 minutes, a number even chemotherapy did not erase from my brain.

My memories of the training leading up to the marathon are fuzzy. Those of the trip to New York with my training partner (who is now my ex-husband) are intact. Cancer may have buried them, but walking through Central Park on a cold November day brought them right to the surface. Poor Eric. He had to listen to me regale him with every detail of the race. He is a patient man and reminded me that his own wife was an avid marathon runner before she got cancer. The rehashing brought back memories for him.

I clearly remember waking at the crack of dawn in a luxurious Manhattan hotel and layering with garments I was willing to "toss" along the way. People warned me that the wait to start could feel like a long winter. They advised me to wear cheap sweats over my running shorts and strip them off when I warmed up. I believe a charity collects them to give to the homeless. A group of us rode together in a limousine to Staten Island, where the race starts. We traveled together from West Palm Beach—carefree, healthy, and determined to come home with bragging rights about "doing New York."

At the start, as 26,000 people cross the Triboro Bridge simultaneously, it starts to sway. I recalled that harmonic motion. Various snippets of the race came back to me: turning north after crossing the Queensboro Bridge, heading up First Avenue to Harlem with people lining the sides of the street and cheering, running into Central Park. At the southwest corner of the park, there was an enormous TV, and the runners could watch themselves turn into the last quarter mile of the race. It was cold and windy that day. I remember wanting to get back to the hotel room for a hot bath and warm food. Why did the memory of the dry bagel and banana at the finish line have to be so sharp? The Mylar® blanket given to all who crossed the finish line was useless to keep in heat as we were forced to trudge north to 72nd Street to exit the park and then limp another mile back to the hotel.

For a few hours, I entertained the idea of trying to whip my little old body back into enough shape to do the New York Marathon again. It would be a joint 50th birthday and congratulations-you-made-the-10-year-mark celebration. I actually bought a new pair of running shoes in the city. We went for an inaugural run. Eric hasn't run since his wife died years ago, and I've been sidelined with bursitis, arthritis, and just about any other "-itis" you might want to add. We started with a really brisk walk to Central Park from our midtown hotel. Then, gingerly, we started to jog. My lungs burned, my knee ached, and Eric had equal complaints. But it felt amazing just to do it. There is no place quite like Central Park on a Sunday morning in the fall. Was it the cold air making my eyes water? I wasn't sure.

If I get up the gumption to train again, at least I will have almost two years. I'll need every minute. It will be a goal, and survivors love goals. Make it to a year, then two, then five, then 10. That mentality never leaves you. Have you ever met a survivor who did not know exactly how many years out they were from their cancer? They may forget how many years they are married, but…

My dilemma: Do I run for the cause or not? Although it would be a great opportunity to raise funds for cancer, I think if I really were ever able to run it, I would want to go back to the anonymity of my pre-cancer marathon. No signs on my back, no asking for donations, just struggling to the finish line—an apt metaphor. I saw a poster on the side of a New York City bus that said it all. It had three bald heads from behind. One had the word "style" across it, the next had "soldier," and the last had "survivor." From behind, they looked identical. I pictured myself crossing that finish line—from behind, just another runner, trying to make the 26.2 miles.

✳ ✳ ✳

New Year's Resolutions
for Survivors

It's that time of year. Time to make resolutions 2010—a new decade, no less. I find the routine ones are boring and overused: lose weight, work out, clean out the closets, be nicer to _____ (fill in the blank with my husband, my wife, my kids, my coworkers, etc.). Does a cancer patient or a cancer survivor have different resolutions?

I still remember my first New Year's as a cancer patient. I approached January 2001 a bald, weak, 40-year-old with braces. I felt someone in my circumstances should have serious New Year's resolutions, but mine were not all deep and meaningful. Getting my braces off was number one on my list. I was determined to convince my orthodontist to humor me. He did. Even cancer patients can be vain.

Weight loss was not in my plans. Cancer stole my appetite and made me skinny. There is no telling if cancer is going to make you thinner or heavier. Each patient is different. Cancer patients are the same as anybody else. They are often bothered by their weight and vow to do something about after their treatments are finished when they feel well enough to make it a realistic resolution. It is hard to hear people say things to cancer patients like, "I wish I had your weight problems!" or "I'd take a little cancer to get rid of this gut!" These people mean no harm. They are simply insensitive. Until they are well enough to follow through, cancer patients' New Year's resolutions must be to be patient enough to wait until they are stronger.

What about that classic New Year's resolution to exercise more and get back into shape? Does it apply to cancer patients? Sure it does. It usually means compromising athletic goals, but not always. Before cancer, I was a marathon runner and a workout maniac. During cancer, taking a walk along the Intracoastal Waterway for a half mile was sufficient to make me feel like I'd run 10 times as long. Climbing one staircase at home was like a half hour on the StairMaster®. My resolution was simply to get outside once a day. Now that I am much healthier and back in shape, I no longer have cancer as an excuse not to do sports. I am amazed at the number of cancer patients I see each day doing physical exercise. They have an internal strength I lacked. There is no reason why cancer patients cannot work out if they feel up to it. Their New Year's resolutions may be to continue what they are already doing. For those cancer patients and survivors who are still not back on their feet, their resolutions must be to listen to their inner self and let it guide them to whatever is best for their own well-being.

The most obvious resolution for cancer patients would be to do whatever it takes to cure themselves. For survivors, it would be to do what they can do diminish their risk of recurrence. Unfortunately, this one is the toughest. We don't have much control over this one, even though we wish we did. Cancer makes us preciously aware of our own mortality. Many survivors "overlive" and try to do everything "right" to guarantee longevity. Certainly, living a healthier lifestyle will help, and it is a good goal.

Now, years into survivorship, I see that old pre-cancer habits have returned. Why? Because cancer doesn't really change our basic personality. As we revert to our old ways, we have the tendency to need the same resolutions as we did before cancer.

So, when the holidays come, survivor or not, a lot of overindulging and frenzied partying is done in anticipation of one calendar day when it is all destined to change. Frankly, I think resolutions are for the birds. We can't change ourselves in a day, a week, or a month. Change is slow, hard work. Putting more pressure on ourselves to accomplish a complete turnaround in that short of a time is unrealistic. For cancer survivors and for the rest of the world, may you live each day in 2010 in a way that makes you proud. Taking it one day at a time is a respected, time-honored approach. Successful baby steps build self-esteem, and self-esteem is the basis for better realizing your resolutions.

My personal resolution: instead of planning resolutions I cannot keep, I resolve to end the cycle that leads up to New Year's resolutions in the first place.

✳ ✳ ✳

Remember, each person has a unique cancer experience. There is no set time designating when survivorship starts or stops. As long as you are comfortable with your own relationship with your cancer, all the other pieces will fall into place. If 30 years later you are still running for "the cure," congratulations to you. If, on the other hand, you fail to remember to put your cancer on a history form at a new doctor's office because it is so far in the past, congratulations to you, too. If your cancer comes back, then dealing with a recurrence comes next.

11

Recurrence

*You gain strength, courage, and confidence by every
experience in which you really stop to look fear in the face.
You are able to say to yourself, "I lived through this horror.
I can take the next thing that comes along."
You must do the thing you think you cannot do.*
—Eleanor Roosevelt

What do cancer patients dread most? Cancer coming back. That is the reason we hold our breath with each scan, blood test, and visit to the doctor. What happens when a recurrence happens? I have no personal experience to guide me on this one, just watching friends and patients go through it. In some ways, recurrence is like a first diagnosis. It can be diagnosed on a routine scan or because of a symptom. Hearing the news still can jump start denial and anger. Treatments for recurrence are discussed once the "best" oncologist is found, and the cycle begins again. The differences between a first-time cancer experience and a recurrence is all about the patient's reaction to the news. For some patients, finding out they have a recurrence does not pack the wallop of the first time. As one-time cancer patients, our brain always has an area that is prepared to hear the diagnosis again. Still, especially for those who had a bad experience the first time around, the news of a recurrence is like a lightening bolt. One woman I know actually vomited in the doctor's office when he told he that her throat cancer had returned. She had so much nausea during her initial treatment that the mere thought of having to deal with it again brought about this visceral reaction.

It's hard not to wonder why you have a recurrence. Patients worry that they were not treated the "right way" the first time around. They blame the doctor or the medical world in general. At the opposite end of the spectrum are patients who worry that they were responsible for the return of their cancer. Either they were not upbeat enough, or failed to eat organic food after their treatments, or give up alcohol, or be more spiritual. The list is endless. Feeling that they are personally to blame for the return of their cancer makes matters worse. Guilt is a useless emotion. It doesn't help solve anything and it makes us feel worse.

Human nature leads us to look for reasons why things happen and to find an absolute explanation. Unfortunately, there aren't a lot of definitive answers to explain recurrence. Whatever caused the first cancer maybe at fault. For instance, a study showed that those of us (me included) who have an inherited genetic alteration that predisposes to more than one cancer actually feel relief knowing why they got cancer. Should they get a recurrence or a second primary cancer, they know why it happened. Most patients are in the dark about what caused their cancer in the first place, let alone a recurrence.

Decisions about treatment a second time around are different. There may not be chemotherapy that is as effective statistically. Radiation may not be an option if the patient has had a maximum dose the first time around. Each of these issues needs to be explored with the treating oncologist. The good news is that there are usually options and modalities to re-treat. The aftermath of treating a recurrence is decidedly different. Patients no longer trust they will be cured. Their anxiety about another recurrence is greater. Some patients begin to feel fatalistic. It is not *if* they get a third recurrence; it is just about *when*. I do know that there are also patients who have an innate positivity about recurrence. Dr. Wendy Harpham, a physician in Texas and a prolific writer and speaker about cancer, recurrence, and survivorship, has been treated eight times for her lymphoma! I am in awe of her ability to deal with her cancer. She has a wonderful husband and two children who help keep her on the path. I refer anyone interested in a wonderful perspective on recurrence to her website to find out more.

In some ways, the cancer acts like other chronic illnesses. Think about heart disease or diabetes. Neither one is really curable. People who suffer from these diseases go through acute bouts with heart attacks, strokes, diabetes-related kidney failure, etc. They live with the risk of another attack, and the possibility of a slow downward course. My own mother had bypass surgery at age 59. Since then, she has had angioplasty and a stroke. Now, she is a diabetic. She understands that she is never really "out of the woods," but there is something else to try if she has another "event."

What happens if your cancer becomes uncontrollable? One of my closest friends, and the woman who was my biggest supporter when I was treated, has never been completely free of her cancer, diagnosed a few years after my own. She has been living with her cancer for more than five years. It will never be behind her, but rather walks beside her every day. We talk about her options for treatment. Her daughters are in high school. She continues to treat to be with them, but she is getting tired. Slowly, she is coming to terms with the prospect of stopping treatment. I support her decisions because I have no idea how I would deal with that situation. As a doctor, I hear patients say things like, "I will *never* take chemotherapy. I would rather die." I see some of those same women in my office, bald and boasting about how they find treatment easier than they thought it would be. The choice to treat, re-treat, or not treat belongs to the patient. That autonomy is paramount.

SURVIVING LIFE

✳ ✳ ✳

Not Again

Last fall, I renovated my home. For months, my house was ripped up and dusty. When the last plank of my Santos Mahogany floor was laid in December, I had a smile from ear to ear. Then, two weeks ago, a water pipe burst under the slab of my home. The water came up through the concrete and ruined my brand new floors. I cried as the last mold-laden plank was removed. All I could think of was, "Not again!"

Coincidentally, I received an email from a survivor who is now facing her husband's newly diagnosed cancer. All she can think of is, "Not again!" How does it feel to have to go through all the testing, waiting, surgery, worried looks on doctors' faces, and so forth for the second time around as a "spectator"?

One of the first thoughts that went through her mind was that she had already "taken the bullet" for the family. Cancer was only supposed to strike once. It made me think of the year when we had two hurricanes in the span of a few weeks. All of us can relate to that feeling.

Then, she reminded me, there is conflict in their different approaches to the disease. She, a survivor, is an information-gatherer who scoured the Internet for "the best" place to be treated and did background checks on all the doctors her husband visited. He, a more laid-back, go-with-the-flow kind of guy, was pretty happy with the first congenial doctor he met. She was a little angry that he wasn't more dogged in his search for the right cancer team. Is that because she felt her intense investigations served her well? What if a less analytical approach ended him up in a doctor's office whose treatments didn't work? Who is responsible? Her, for not pushing him to be more aggressive, or him, for being too passive? There is a huge chance that their conflicting approaches will impact their relationship if they don't resolve them. Ultimately, it is the patient's choice, not the survivor's choice. Luckily for this couple, he was amenable to letting her do the legwork and went along with most of her decisions.

Having the survivor take charge is not that unusual. I spoke with quite a few double-cancer couples, and it is common for one to take a back seat to the other. Most of the time, the second one to get cancer felt that the first was more experienced and would be better at making some of the critical decisions based on their own cancer treatments. This thinking may be flawed. Every cancer is different, and every treatment is tweaked to be the right one for each patient. Thus, what was good for the goose may not be so good for the gander, so to speak.

During the treatments for the new cancer, who is there to support the survivor? The pressure for the survivor to be strong for the new cancer patient is intense. Any survivor will tell you that going to oncology visits, being in hospitals (even as a visitor), sitting in chemotherapy infusion rooms, or walking into a radiation center all evoke strong emotions. Sometimes, memories that have been suppressed for years start to surface. As the major caregiver, there isn't a lot of time to get therapy or go to a support group. Besides, going to a support group can be as traumatic for the survivor-caregiver as not.

Probably the hardest part of going through the cancer experience a second time around as an observer is the fear that the spouse won't be as lucky and won't be cured. Watching a loved one die is hard enough, but it is harder still when you are a cancer survivor. It isn't all that different from the survivor guilt experienced by plane crash passengers.

With cancer affecting over a third of our population, there will be more and more cases of double-cancer families. Many programs are already available to help "single" cancer survivors. I have no doubt that they will expand to cover these issues in the future.

As I sit writing this column, I am staying at a friend's house, until the mold remediators can check out my home, and then I will select new floors. Facing the construction anew doesn't thrill me, but I'd rather be doing that than facing cancer and thinking, "Not again."

※ ※ ※

In case my message was unclear, let me state that your cancer is your cancer. You can be as aggressive as you want and treat as many times as you want. On the other hand, no doctor, friend, or family member should badger you into treatment if you have decided to live life without more intervention. If allowing your cancer to take its natural course is your choice, then you will face what may come next: end-of-life decisions.

12

Death

While I thought that I was learning how to live,
I have been learning how to die.
—Leonardo da Vinci

What happens if cancer returns and can no longer be treated, or the patient elects to stop treatment? There is no easy way to tell a patient that they cannot be cured of their disease. Miracles do happen, but not commonly. Part of the cancer experience may be dealing with end-of-life issues. My own husband was a widower when I met him. His wife died at age 45 of colon cancer. He has taught me most of what I know about dying of cancer.

In our society, it is hard to talk about death and incurable illnesses. Doctors and patients alike feel uncomfortable discussing it. Other cultures accept death as part of the life cycle. Usually, they are cultures without medical care at their fingertips. I believe that our developed nation could learn from the experiences of undeveloped countries regarding the dying process. It saddens me to learn about cancer patients dying in the middle of "courageous battles" with their disease. Why? It implies that either they or their physicians did not take steps to prepare for death. I realize it is a person's right to "fight until the end," but I am not a fan of the war analogy. It is too violent for me. Also, I have heard so many stories about patients who went into the hospital "riddled with cancer" and were given a dose of chemotherapy, only to succumb the next day. We tend to value heroic efforts and feel like "losers" if we give up. That perception must change. Thoughtful conversations need to take place with patients and family members to determine if aggressive measures are appropriate.

The hospice movement is growing by leaps and bounds in America. I believe this is due to the paradigm shift in addressing death. If a cancer death is unavoidable, it behooves us to treat the patient with dignity and keep the person as comfortable as possible. Also, hospice is invaluable in helping the family to prepare for the patient's death and to get the support they need afterward. End-of-life planning is integral to hospice care. When I was a freshman at Georgetown University, my theology class addressed death and dying. On the first day of studies, we were asked to describe the way we would like to die. Virtually every student wrote about dying in their sleep at age 90 (this was the 1970s when that was a very ripe old age) with no pain. As the semester passed along, we read about closure before dying and the cons of sudden death for those left behind. I started volunteering for a hospice in Washington, DC at the same time. I got to see firsthand the amazing way hospice workers helped with the dying process. The final exam for my theology class was again to describe how we wanted to die to see if it differed from the past. Most students still wanted to die quickly and painlessly. I wrote about dying from cancer in hospice care. To this day, I am convinced that if I die that way, it will be with grace, and when the time comes for me to die, both my family and I will be ready. I don't claim to be more evolved than other people, but I watched my own dad die of heart disease, and my mother still feels that she has "unfinished business" with him. I wonder if that would be the case had he had a slower, more "organized" death.

Good or Bad, We Die

My future father-in-law died this week. He had prostate cancer. When I met Hank (not his real name), he was introduced as a "health nut," a 70-something-year-old man who'd eaten sushi for decades before it was popular. He never drank alcohol or smoked cigarettes and barely ate fat. Hank was thin, but had muscles of steel from daily spinning classes and running. His house has pictures of him running marathons with his daughter. Sarah (also not her real name) is Hank's wife of more than 50 years. They had a wonderful, loving marriage. They met at age 14 and were the most devoted couple I'd encountered in my life. Hank died at Hospice by the Sea. The staff was amazing with him, his wife, and the whole family. It was the best end to a difficult situation. Hank lived with his cancer for a long time. Had he not been in fantastic physical shape, we would have lost him a lot earlier.

The morning of the funeral, I couldn't sleep. It bothered me that we lost our "Poppy" when he wasn't finished with being a husband, father, grandfather, and mentor. I was depressed that all his efforts to be "good" couldn't save him. Why is it that the adage "Bad things happen to good people" rings true? Every day, I encounter people who don't take care of themselves. They are overweight and out of shape. They drink, smoke, and abuse their bodies. They take a list of medications as long as my arm. Yet, they are older than Hank and are still going strong.

Then, I remember my mother reminding me that life is not fair. Death is not fair. Good people die, and bad people live. I am reminded that we should never really label someone as good or bad, because we are all equal. I believe that you should not judge others lest you be judged. We are all guilty of judging others. When you are patiently waiting for a parking spot and a person coming from the other direction zooms in ahead of you, anger erupts. You decide that person is bad. Is it really "bad" to steal a parking spot? It might be rude or selfish, but is the person that does a rude or selfish behavior really a bad person? At times like this, I admit I am as guilty of these minor transgressions as everyone else. But I am convinced that I am essentially a good person. So was Hank.

Luckily, we are a forgiving society. Or maybe we just have a short memory. Look at all the "bad people" who have a made a comeback, their "badness" forgiven and mostly forgotten. Bill Clinton was vilified for his womanizing, and yet he is by Hillary's side, traveling the world and getting paid millions to speak. At the moment, Mr. Madoff is a bad man. I agree that his behavior was abhorrent, but to his wife and family, I bet he is a good man. I tell my children that if they turn out to be axe murderers, I won't like them, but I will always love them.

Back to Hank. His daughter died almost seven years ago. She was definitely a "good " person. Everyone tells me she was a fantastic wife, mother, and daughter. Unfortunately, she is another example of how cancer doesn't care if you are good or bad. Some survivors believe that if they devote themselves to helping others and live a "good, clean life," they will be protected from recurrence. If only it were that easy. Good or bad, we live, and good or bad, we die.

As I held Hank's still-warm hand, I grieved a "good" life over. I chose to remember our last Thanksgiving meal. Hank was so happy to have the family together, joking, laughing, and making memories. Eric and I really wanted Hank to be a part of our special day. He will be, just not in person.

✳ ✳ ✳

SURVIVING LIFE

Hospice Care Is a Benefit to All

November is National Hospice Month. I was introduced to the hospice movement when, as a junior at Georgetown University in the late 1970s, I volunteered at a hospice in Washington, DC. Little did I know that what was a fledgling concept 30 years ago was destined to become a mainstay of treating the terminally ill in the 21st century.

The hospice movement was founded in England to help cancer patients "die with dignity." More specifically, hospice care was conceived as a way for terminally ill patients to plan the end of their life. Everything from pain management to funeral plans falls under the umbrella of hospice care. Dying at home surrounded by family is central to the concept. In-patient facilities do exist, but hospice care is designed to take place at home.

Letting patients control their death is a new concept for most of us. In order to do so, most hospices help to compose a document called an "advance directive." Advance directives spell out the patient's wishes in detail, thereby ensuring that the patient is treated as he would want to be and avoiding family disagreements and misunderstandings when the patient is no longer able to communicate his needs. Commonly, hospice patients are referred by their treating physician. Patients are often admitted to a facility at first, both to stabilize their pain control and to allow the family time to set up the home for hospice care. Keeping ill patients comfortable at home in familiar surrounding and utilizing therapists and social workers to assist in preparing the families are key elements of hospice care. Even though family members and loved ones are the main caregivers, most hospices use visiting nurses to check on patients, and many have physicians who make house calls. A fully evolved hospice only uses an in-patient facility for "respite care" when caregivers need a break. Hospice is not intended as a place to send patients when death is imminent. However, in America, many people are still not comfortable watching a loved one die at home. Our in-patient facilities often turn into a place where families bring their loved one to die. Once the patient has died, hospice stays involved, offering bereavement counseling and long-term support groups.

When hospice is used as intended, it can make an enormous difference in the death experience, both for the patient and the family. Hospice of Palm Beach County is one of the largest in the United States. Their services include everything from palliative care to aromatherapy and imagery work. Mitch and Bobbi recently benefitted from its programs. The couple met and married at age 21. Mitch was diagnosed with cancer in his 40s, and just months after their 31st wedding anniversary, at age 52, he knew he was dying. He decided to plan the end of his life to make it easier for everyone. He felt it was better to have the details worked out ahead of time than to leave a lot of important decision-making to his soon-to-be widow. Making his wishes known took pressure off his family. He stated what he did and did not want done as part of his care. Most importantly, he helped his wife plan her future without him. The hospice staff was comfortable facilitating these discussions. By the time Mitch died, Bobbi was well-prepared and found peace watching his suffering come to an end.

So, during this month, even if you don't have a terminal illness or have a family member with one, it is not too early to explore an end-of-life plan. A hospice referral should be made when the patient has less than six months to live in the best estimation of the doctor. Unfortunately, the average hospice stay is less than a few weeks. It is almost impossible to do the work necessary to prepare both patient and family in such a short time. If all of us work to make hospice care the norm, it will be a win-win healthcare option: it will provide better care at a lower cost and bring families together when they need it most.

✳ ✳ ✳

Living Wills

My father died last week. A part of me died with him. It was the part of me that innocently believed I understood end-of-life issues. From my first introduction to the concept of hospice care during college, I thought I would have no trouble applying it to my own family. If my dad had suffered from cancer, it might have been different, but he had heart disease, and it never occurred to me that there would be a need to involve hospice. Unfortunately, there was ambiguity in my dad's living will. The last few weeks of his life opened my eyes to what can happen when very ill patients and their families and doctors face impossibly hard decisions.

A month before, I invited my mom and dad to a charity event. My father looked unwell and was short of breath after only a few steps. He was suffering from congestive heart failure. Within days, he faced a catch 22 situation: go home to wait to die, or have open-heart surgery with a high risk of either dying during or right after surgery. He made the decision to proceed with surgery despite the odds. The medical interventions my dad received were unparalleled in their quality, once again proving to me that there is top-notch care here in Palm Beach County. Unfortunately, despite skilled surgeons, a great intensive care unit at Bethesda Heart Institute, and wonderful nursing care, my father's 81-year-old body could not bounce back from surgery. The doctors were optimistic and yet they were unable to wean him off the ventilator, and soon, despite a good-as-new heart, his other organs failed. We dug through his files at home to find his living will to guide us. Once found, we believed that it would be straightforward to see that his wishes about what he wanted done and not done were followed. This was not the case. The paper we were using was an "antique" version of a living will. It granted power to his attending physician to decide when my father was "terminally ill" and used the time frame of "imminent death" to guide us to turn off life support. Neither doctors nor family members wanted to "play God" to make those determinations. I discovered that there is no clear demarcation between waiting for a medical miracle and deciding that interventions are not prolonging life, but prolonging the dying process.

They say the devil is in the details, and this may be the case with living wills. My father's living will was fairly "cookie cutter." It dated back many years. Even now, I was under the impression that all you need to do to have a living will is do an online search of the words and a bunch of websites pop up. You download the living will of your choice, sign it in front of a witness, and voila! Wrong. I ended up doing a little research *after* my father's death to discover the ins and outs of living wills. Now, I feel slightly more informed and ready to offer some limited insight. Please do not take my words as those of an expert, and seek one out as needed when preparing your own living will.

So what is a living will? In 1985 (updated again in 1989), a bill was passed called the Uniform Rights of the Terminally Ill Act. Almost every state in the union has adopted it. This act allows people to make preparation for a time when they may be too sick or unable to make their desires known about medical interventions. A living will is a type of health-care directive or advance directive. These documents (or videos) are designed to take guesswork out of deciding what a patient wants done to them in certain medical situations when they are rendered unable to communicate their needs effectively. It can address specific wishes about medical procedures like receiving nutrition through a tube or hydration by IV when in a coma, terminally ill, or on life support. A living will or health-care directive can be written by any individual, witnessed by someone over 18, and distributed to appropriate friends and/or relatives to have at hand should the need arise to use it. Alternatively, power of attorney or designation of health-care proxy status, is a legal term referring to a person selected to speak on your behalf and make decisions for you should you be rendered unable, as opposed to following directives you have already spelled out beforehand.

Following are a few suggestions about these documents, which I gleaned from reading more about them online. Do not place all the power to make decisions for your loved one in the hands of one of the attending physicians. It places them in a conflicted position. They may not know the patient as well as the family and may have other agendas guiding them. Try to make these documents as detailed and specific as possible. Vague words such as "terminal" or "imminent" may seem appropriate when writing a living will, but they become open for interpretation when being applied in an emotion-charged atmosphere. Remember that the living will is for the patient's needs to be met, not the doctors' nor those of the family members. There may be someone who does not agree with what the patient decided to do, but they must respect the wishes of their loved one.

In my father's case, we finally called in hospice only hours before he died. It was definitely worthwhile. He passed in a serene, dignified way. Ultimately, my father is at peace, and we are grieving the loss of a very special man. He was so fond of teaching and did it mostly by example. Daddy, how true to your personality that even in death, you taught an amazing life lesson to those of us closest to you.

* * *

Healing from the death of a loved one takes a very long time. It does not matter if the person died quickly or slowly. If we could establish a good etiquette for dying, death, and beyond, the healing might be gentler. My proposal for such an etiquette comes next.

13

Cancer Etiquette

What you must dare is to be yourself.
—Dag Hammarskjold

From diagnosis to death and beyond, most of us feel completely uncomfortable around cancer. We lack a defined cancer etiquette. We don't know how to talk to a cancer patient. We aren't sure of what to send as a gift when someone is diagnosed with cancer. Our fallback, flowers and chocolates, are not the best choices. Flowers die in a few days, and cancer patients may not feel in the mood to eat sweets. So how do we learn how to navigate cancer?

My best advice is simple. The person with cancer is the same person you knew the day before you found out they had cancer. I encourage you to talk to them just as you would have before you both knew the diagnosis. My least-favorite memories were those of people tilting their heads to the side and putting on an overconcerned expression, then asking me how I felt. I could feel how uncomfortable they were. To this day, I am asked, "How are you, really?" on a daily basis. Translation: "Are you cured? Is your cancer back?" A friend with chronic cancer moved to another country in part because she was sick and tired of these questions. I don't blame her. However, I am determined to help educate about cancer etiquette. One of the first questions I would ask people who are uncomfortable around a cancer patient is: "How do you talk to them if they had a heart attack? Or diabetes?"

As for gifts, there are so many useful things to give. Stuffed animals with ribbons are cute, but usually end up on a shelf or donated. Inspirational books, tapes, or CDs are nice. But what if the patient is not really spiritual. Head coverage is dicey, but popular. A pretty scarf is nice, but beware of hats and wigs. They need to be sized and fitted. I detested hats and to this day have trouble with head scarves after wearing them nonstop for months. Excuse me if I seem ruthless, but few of us have the nerve to expose the truth. The risk of buying the "wrong" item is no different than gift-giving on other occasions. I invented a few items that I feel are excellent to give a cancer patient. One is a nightgown and pillowcase to help with night sweats so common during treatment. Most women will go through a temporary (or even permanent) menopause, fondly referred to as "chemopause" due to the sensitivity of ovaries to chemotherapy. These quick-dry gifts make getting through the night easier. I also came up with a shirt with tabs at the shoulders to access a port (an indwelling IV in the chest). They say necessity is the mother of invention. I was so cold at the chemotherapy infusion center from exposing my chest that I came up with this one just to keep warm. The list of "good" gifts is long. Whatever you give, if done with sincerity and support, not with fear, will feel right.

SURVIVING
LIFE

How Do You Talk to
a Cancer Patient?

How do you talk to a cancer patient? A question I am asked almost daily. Usually, it comes from the patient in stirrups in the exam room. "Doctor, can I ask you something personal?" My mind races. Is the person going to probe me about my divorce, my love life, my professional partnership, or ask about some alternative sexual practice? (All of these have happened, for sure). Then, the person goes on to explain that a friend or relative was just diagnosed with cancer, and that person is afraid to call the friend. "You are the expert," the person contends. "Tell me what I should say. How do I talk to him?" The person's tone borders on desperate. The same question comes in by email or phone message so often that I have finally come to believe that the problem is bigger than I originally thought.

So how do you talk to a cancer patient? My advice is simple. You talk to a cancer patient the same way you talked to that person the week before the diagnosis. The person had cancer then, but just didn't know it yet. Easy for me to suggest, but hard for someone feeling uncomfortable to do. Keep in mind that the cancer patient has her own original identity. Once the cancer diagnosis is made, the person becomes a patient or a survivor forever, not merely your spouse, friend, or colleague. I liken it to Eve in the Garden of Eden. Once partaken of the forbidden fruit, her innocence was gone forever.

The problem is usually not with the patient, but with whoever is trying to talk to the patient. This is not to say that receiving a cancer diagnosis is easy on the ears for the recipient. But the patient quickly becomes immersed in the world of cancer and its treatment. It helps the patient adjust to the diagnosis. A cancer patient goes through fairly predictable stages of behavior in order to cope. The first, denial, is the stage where the patient's brain doesn't really let the diagnosis sink in. Denial gives the patient energy to move through the surgery, radiation, or chemotherapy. Over time, the cancer patient experiences many other stages that end with acceptance and accommodation. Patients learn to incorporate the disease and its fallout into their lives. Luckily, most cancer patients are offered counseling to help them transition.

Friends and relatives have a different cancer experience unless they, themselves, are also survivors. When they hear that their loved one has cancer, they are often shocked and saddened. But many other thoughts and emotions happen. They are scared. If cancer struck so close to them, then it might strike them. As a society, we tend to ignore our mortality, and when someone close to us gets a life-threatening disease, we are forced to admit that we are also susceptible.

Friends also feel helpless. They cannot cure the cancer for their friend. They cannot undergo the treatments for their friend. Instead, they send things to let the cancer patient know they care. These expressions of love and support are great to a point. From this cancer patient's perspective, cards and handwritten notes are the best. They can be saved and reread at a later date. The notes telling me I was in someone's thoughts and prayers were perfect. I didn't particularly like store-bought cards with the metaphor of fighting a battle together or being on the same team in a tough match, but for some cancer patients, these might be the right approach. This is where your knowledge of your friend's likes and dislikes helps. Tailor the card to your friend's personality. If the patient is a sarcastic person, a soft and mushy card won't do the trick.

Many people feel that sending a card or note is not enough to express their support. They want to send a gift. Along come the flowers and boxes of candy. I still remember my oncologist, deathly allergic to lilies, was unable to come into my hospital room to examine me until the flower arrangements were removed. The displays were beautiful, but cut flowers were destined to die within days, and I was not in the mood to see that happen. Besides, vases are hard to transport home from the hospital without spilling. I donated all but the orchids to the nurses. Hint: orchids bloom for a long time and then bloom over and over again. They are a perfect plant gift.

Candy is a common gift. Unfortunately, many cancer patients don't have a good appetite. Candy may look great and smell delicious, but it isn't the best food or nutrition for a cancer patient. On the other hand, it is very good to give visitors as a snack. I also offered the rest of the candy to the nurses as a late-night treat.

Are there other ways to communicate love and support to a cancer patient if the few most common are not suitable? Of course. The food chain that my friends did for the entire time I was in chemotherapy was invaluable. Every other night, a different friend delivered dinner to my doorstep. Amazing. My family ate like kings. We had everything from lasagna to tenderloin, and usually there was a special "kid-friendly" item thrown in for my children. Some friends included a plate of home-baked cookies or fruit salad for dessert. Just the love that went into the preparation of these meals made me feel better.

Another friend took my children out every afternoon that I had chemotherapy and did not bring them back until she was sure I was tucked in bed and prepared for the onslaught of my babies. They went to the park, made ceramic mugs, ate pizza, or took in a movie. It was a terrific expression of love.

The list of nice, thoughtful, and useful things you can do for someone who has cancer is very long. Just put yourself in that person's shoes for a moment, imagine what you would want to make the difficult times easier, and you will figure out just what to do for your friend. If not, you could pick up the phone and ask. Which brings me all the way back to the original question: How do you talk to a cancer patient? Answer: How would you like to be talked to as a cancer patient? Would you want to be pitied or the recipient of a doom-and-gloom attitude? Would you want someone to cheer you up with a rah-rah spirit or sit quietly by your side holding your hand? Each person is different. If you are close to the patient, then you should understand that person's basic personality and go from there. If you are not close, I advise a short, simple note, and there is scientific data to back it up. A study was done showing that patients who were prayed for had better outcomes (even if they didn't know they were being prayed for). So with your words and prayers, you are part of the road to recovery.

SURVIVING LIFE

✳ ✳ ✳

Prayer

What gift do you give a cancer patient? When I was in the hospital for cancer surgery, my room was full of flower arrangements. It looked like a funeral parlor. The flowers were beautiful, but died within days—not to mention that my oncologist is allergic to lilies, and I had to have them removed before she could set foot in my room each day. Friends brought me candy. I was too sick to eat it, but it made a good snack to offer visitors. Some well-meaning individual sent me a 500-page book about natural cancer remedies. At night, when I couldn't sleep, I flipped absentmindedly through the pages, but couldn't concentrate long enough to read an entire chapter. *People* and *Cosmo* were easier on the eyes and brain.

I arrived home to a shopping bag full of cards, notes, and letters. Some funny. Some serious. Some Hallmark®. Some homemade. A good portion of them said the same thing. Not only was I in my friends' thoughts, I was definitely in their prayers.

I was a practicing Jew at the time of my diagnosis. I still am. My then-husband, who had converted to my faith before we married, decided to revert to Christianity at about the same time I was diagnosed. In retrospect, I think he was turning back to his roots as a source of comfort. I was too sick to protest.

When he decided that we should expose our four children to both religions, I found myself attending church regularly. This religious upheaval turned out to be a great thing. Why? Because of prayer. When the family went to synagogue, I discovered that we were being prayed for. When we went to church, both friends and strangers stopped me to tell me they were actively praying for my recovery and for my family. We became a multi-faith family. I am proud of it. Eventually, I wrote a book with our minister to help congregants of the Presbyterian Church across the United States going through the cancer experience. This cemented my relationship with the spectrum of Judeo-Christian religions.

At the time, I did not really consider the meaning of all these prayers. I knew that Jews said a prayer of healing called a Misheberach. The congregation is invited to pray for sick people in general or for a specific sick person. In the Christian faith, I was prayed for both at church and in private. Months after I returned to work, I discovered that a church in the Florida Panhandle devoted an entire service to praying for my health.

Were these prayers helpful? Did they make me recover faster or easier? Am I still in remission today because of them? Who knows? What isn't known is if I would still be here if no one had prayed for me. Some of my atheist friends assure me that there is no scientific evidence proving that praying for someone makes a difference. One gentleman, a real skeptic, laughed in my face. "You can't really believe that prayer makes a difference?" His voice was dripping with sarcasm. At first glance, I admit that without faith, there is no easy way to explain it. It is one thing to pray with the sick person aware of it and in the same room. There is that little catch of explaining how praying from the other side of the state for someone you don't even know can possibly impact their outcome.

Recently, a study was done about prayer and cancer survival. While there is no hard data to show that prayer altered the ultimate outcome of patients, those patients who were spiritual (self-defined) did cope better with their disease and reported better "well-being" during treatment. One study in the 1980s about patients in a cardiac care unit indicated that patients who were prayed for actually had increased survival and improved outcome. Patients who were prayed for, even by strangers, and even unaware that they were being prayed for, appeared to fare better than those for whom no prayers were spoken. Unfortunately, a follow-up study at Harvard in 2006 refuted this data. They had three groups of patients undergoing cardiac surgery. One group knew they were being prayed for. Two groups were told they might or might not be prayed for. Prayers were said for one of these last two groups. The three groups, that is those who knew they were prayed for, those who didn't know and were prayed for, and those who were not prayed for, all had similar rates of complications and hospital courses.

Does prayer make a difference? For those skeptics, let me ask the converse. Will it really hurt to have someone pray for you? I doubt it. More studies need to be done, but there was a time when the world was assumed to be flat, so it wouldn't surprise me to find out that prayer has value. Almost seven years later, back at work, I ask myself, "Am I here because I was lucky? Is it because I had great health care? Is it because someone prayed for me? Or is it all of the above?" Patients whom I haven't seen in a long time come in and comment on how good I look. "We prayed for you," they said. I know that it made a difference even if I can't explain how or why.

The best part of that shopping bag full of cards is I still have it. I can read the notes over and over again to help me through hard times. The prayers are always there when I need them.

So, what do you give a cancer patient? A prayer. An expression of hope.

SURVIVING LIFE

✳ ✳ ✳

Cancer and Obituaries

I can't remember when I started reading the obituaries. I didn't even turn to that page before I got cancer. During treatment, the newspaper was a welcome distraction, and I actually read it instead of scanning the headlines the way I did when I was a working mother of four. The first time I looked at the obituaries, it was out of curiosity. How did other cancer patient's families announce the passing of their loved one? What an eye-opener!

The obituaries with a photo caught my eye first. Most of the pictures were pretty dated. I envisioned a grieving spouse, frantically searching for a nice picture to put in the paper, going through drawers of photos from family get-togethers, Aunt Jean's 80th birthday celebration, or a long lost high school yearbook.

Virtually every obituary about a cancer patient had the same theme: the patient died after a long (or short) *courageous battle* with the disease. Visions of war were planted in my brain. Not a bad metaphor, but personally I would never use those words. I told my family that, should I die of my cancer and they put a line like that in my obituary, I would come from the other side to give them what-for.

Nobody has been able to enlighten me about the source of the war metaphor. After reading as many cancer books as possible, written from all sorts of perspectives, it occurs to me that our cultural heritage and stereotypes encourage aggression against an invader, and that is how most of us see our cancer. Almost all patients, but men in particular, feel threatened by their cancer. The hormone testosterone is much higher in men than in women, and it evokes a fight response. I suspect that if you took a poll of average female cancer patients in whom estrogen is the dominant hormone, the cancer battle may be quite different. I don't mean to imply that women's will to survive cancer is any less strong, just that their approach may be less direct than the war metaphor.

When a woman is faced with a challenge as formidable as cancer, she will tend to seek support among her closest friends and experience the disease process as part of her cure. Communicating with other cancer patients and sharing their stories is key to survival. Another difference I see between men and women and their approach to cancer is that men see the problem as a finite issue. They want a few definitive answers. "Why did I get cancer? What is the most effective treatment? What are the survival statistics?" They want to treat and move on. They are seeking a path back to the normality they had before cancer. Women ask the same questions, but add a few more. They want to be involved with their health-care team. They want to explore most all avenues before making the final decisions about treatment. I have consulted with patients who sought out at least five opinions before deciding on the right course of treatment. I think this is because women need to make a connection with their caregiver that makes them feel not only cared for, but cared about. Women are more prone to find a "new normal" and to incorporate the cancer into it.

After cancer, the majority of men are ready to put the disease behind them. If they need to battle again at a later date, so be it. Women continue to identify with their cancer for long periods of time, if not forever. Survivor status may come to define them and alter their lives forever. The best advocates, fundraisers, and educators are survivors who feel compelled to get the word out. Contributions such as those made by Nancy Brinker, founder of the Susan G. Komen Foundation, are incredible because she is a survivor with the drive to give back to other cancer patients, their families, and friends. I consider Nancy a role model and a friend. She helped me through my struggles by example. If I could touch even a fraction of the people she has, I would consider myself a success.

I mean no disrespect to cancer patients who are very aggressive about their cancer fight. Probably those same patients had more aggressive personalities before cancer. They are the ones seen wearing T-shirts at cancer events that say things like "Cancer Sucks." I wonder if they do better or survive longer. I am not aware of any data on personality sub-types and survival. I find fighting and intense confrontation really uncomfortable. Getting riled up for a fight against cancer is as stressful a thought as the cancer itself. Better to find a way to be inspired by cancer to make a mark on the planet. The less-aggressive cancer patients, like me, would wear a T-shirt that would say something like "Cancer Can Be the Answer." Suffice to say that whatever works for a particular individual to get them through treatment is the right approach for that person.

Back to the obituaries: Whether I die from a recurrence of this cancer, a different cancer, or something altogether unrelated, I want the record to reflect that my relationship with cancer was symbiotic and my obituary to be a tribute to my cancer.

No discussion of obituaries would be complete without a brief mention of funerals and memorial services. Most funerals I have attended are for the living. Unless the deceased requested something special, it is up to the remaining family members to determine what is best. Some of you might remember the cult movie *Harold and Maude* where the 70-something-year-old Maude meets the 20-something-year-old Harold because they both attend funerals for entertainment. The movie is a spoof on death, but the central message is positive. Death may take us away from this earth, but a life lived fully should engender only short-term mourning. The goal to remain alive without quality may not be right for some people. I once met Ruth Gordon, the actress who played Maude. She, like her character, lived life to the fullest and was ready for what could befall her. At my funeral…take that back, I don't want a funeral. When my ultimate day of rest gets here, I request a reception. Please serve Toll House cookies and play Motown, and I will know you got the message right.

❊ ❊ ❊

It is going to take a long time before we feel as comfortable with cancer as we do with other diseases, but I predict it will happen. Younger generations who see their parents and friends' parents surviving cancer (for the most part) already are more comfortable talking about it, seeing it, and living it. Eventually, books like this will be passé as we all learn to accept cancer as "just another disease" and put it in its place.

Conclusion

How did one six letter word, C-A-N-C-E-R, get so much power? I don't know. The three-letter word W-A-R came first, and it really packs a wallop. But I don't even think that people are afraid of war as much as they are afraid of cancer. Why? Because unless one of your loved ones is enlisted or serving, war still seems a little distant and unreal. Cancer does not feel as distant or unreal as war. It feels like an "equal opportunity killer" to most of us. Before the 20th century, C-A-N-C-E-R was synonymous with D-E-A-T-H. Then again, infections were also synonymous with D-E-A-T-H. Now, infections can be treated, although some are lethal. We are no longer as afraid of infections, but the cancer stigma remains. Probably because cancer, unlike an infection or a heart attack, rarely kills quickly. The suffering and drawn-out nature of most cancer deaths gave it a nasty reputation. That reputation is changing. A paradigm shift of putting cancer in its place is happening. Not minimizing how devastating it can be, not giving it more power than it deserves, but letting it fit into each person's life as it will.

SURVIVING LIFE

✳ ✳ ✳

Little Word, Big Impact

My youngest son looked up at me, batting his angelic blue eyes with long lashes. I suspected what was coming.

"Can I have this new video game? Pretty, please?" Bat, bat, bat.

"What is it rated?" I asked. The question was unnecessary. I knew if he had picked a game rated "E" (appropriate for everyone), he wouldn't have started the flirtatious behavior. He would have plunked down his allowance at the cash register.

"T (appropriate for teens). But that's just for violence and a few bad words. Mom, I swear there's no sex in it. Can I get it?"

"Why can't you find an E-rated game?" I asked. I already knew the answer.

"They are so boring and babyish. Besides mom, there isn't anything in this game that I haven't seen before. Just some blood, stabbings, and gunshot wounds."

Unfortunately, I understood. Today, the violence and bad language in media is mind-numbing. To deny my son the video game would certainly send a reinforcing message about my personal feelings regarding these topics. I hate them. But he is already perfectly aware of how I feel about them. Trying to insulate him from violence and bad language is like trying to put a fence around the ocean. Besides, if I deny him exposure to these video games, they become a forbidden fruit, enticing him to partake.

What does this have to do with cancer? Hang in there, and I will explain it. The youth of today is overexposed to violence. Getting shot and killed is no big deal in a movie or a game. The highest-grossing movies at the box office are full of death and destruction. It is shocking how unaffected we are by violent death. Someone gets shot, too bad. Someone gets taken down in a drug bust, no big deal. How can that possibly be? Maybe because the game or movie fails to show the fallout. They don't enter the victim's life to see the impact the death has on the family. Nobody gives thought to the father who won't be walking through the door to dinner or the mother who will never get a birthday kiss from her son again. Or worse, the dead person is portrayed as such a lowlife that they have no close relationships that will suffer when he is gone.

Unlike the way we have become almost indifferent to sudden violent death, cancer deaths remain tragic and poignant. Media portrayal of cancer death is almost always slow and painful. The family is distraught and bereft. The reality is that cancer is about as random as a drive-by shooting. The latter is fodder for video games and headlines, and the former is not. I haven't seen a headline "Another Young Life Lost to Cancer." So why is it that violent deaths are plastered on the front page of the newspaper while cancer deaths are relegated to the obituaries page?

Someone pointed out to me that it is socioeconomic or cultural. If you were raised in a place where violent deaths were a daily reality, you would be far more afraid of a bullet than cancer because there was a real chance you might be killed in a random attack. In gang communities, cancer seems a distant prospect given the fact that so many members never make it past young adulthood. On the other hand, the middle and upper classes, who have never even driven into a "dangerous" part of town where random violence occurs, have a higher likelihood of being exposed to cancer through a family member's ordeal. They are petrified of suffering from cancer and don't even consider dying from a gunshot or stab wound.

It boils down to fear of the known. For many of us, it is fear of even the word cancer. Some people who have cancer don't even want the word written or spoken aloud. They refer to their disease as "my illness." Is there a way to lessen the impact of this one word? If we can take what is verboten and make it commonplace, like violent death in the media, maybe it would not have the power to hurt us so much. How can that be done? For starters, reeducating the public about cancer. Currently, a lot of press is given to prevention and early detection. Copious information is also available on the Internet. None of it has succeeded in disconnecting the word cancer from the emotion we call dread. As a survivor and a physician, I feel there needs to be a campaign to demystify cancer. Not make it blasé or minimize how serious it is, but create a paradigm shift in the public's perception of the disease. For a good portion of us who have been treated, that has already happened. Before I was diagnosed, I was petrified of cancer. Now, realizing that there is usually a finite time when a person's life is in upheaval during treatment but then renormalizes, I would opt to do it again over dying from a gunshot wound.

It probably is too late to change the way baby boomers view cancer—as a death sentence. But for the adolescents of today, there is time. Perhaps a video game in which cancer is the bad guy. Cancer strikes, sucking "life points" out of the player. When appropriate surgery, chemotherapy, radiation, or immunotherapy is administered, the player is brought back and triumphs. Then, when my future grandson asks me about buying the newest cancer video game, I will know we have succeeded in our mission to desensitize cancer.

About my son and the violent video game. I decided to let him exercise his independent decision-making skills. He bought the game. As I suspected, he played it once, found it far-less-interesting than he thought it would be, and decided to exchange it for a soccer game.

✳ ✳ ✳

When told she has a 50/50 chance of carrying the gene that caused my cancer, my 15-year old daughter put it all into perspective. "I hope I have the gene," she said. "Why on earth would you hope for that?" I asked. "Look how great you are, Mom. I want to be just like you!"

While I would not wish cancer on anyone, I wouldn't wish any debilitating disease on anyone. Having said that, cancer is just cancer. And should you be diagnosed, you now know what comes next, and that is the first step to putting cancer in its place.

Appendix

Dr. Melanie Bone:
From 'pleaser' to crusader
'Someone Was Sending a Message: Your Work Is Not Done'
By Carolyn Susman
Palm Beach Post Staff Writer
Thursday, October 12, 2006

All her life, she was a "pleaser," someone who shied away from confrontation.

She lived a "totally sheltered life" and married her first husband at 25 because "I was afraid to move to another city by myself."

She was "a brainiac" with so little self-awareness that she still wore clothes from high school when she arrived in West Palm Beach in 1991.

Then Dr. Melanie Bone got cancer.

And, she says, she woke up.

Breast cancer took both her breasts and her energy during chemotherapy and radiation— but it gave her something important, says Dr. Bone, an obstetrician/gynecologist.

It focused her life.

"I found myself at 40 with this life-threatening disease and waking up, all at the same time. I had thought I was a nobody; I was very naive. I was smart, but I didn't know what Phi Beta Kappa meant (when she was chosen to be a member of the prestigious academic society). I started to grow up. I started to get self-esteem."

It seems odd for a successful doctor to admit so many vulnerabilities. But Bone, 46, says she's not unlike many of her patients.

"I see in my practice every day amazing women who fly below the radar screen and at 40 to 45 become self-aware and are really good people without the benefit of their spouses," she says.

A family filled with physicians

Melanie Bone comes from a family of driven professionals. Her father, Jesse, is a psychiatrist. Her brother, her uncle and her grandfather were all doctors. Her sister, Lori-Nan—also a cancer survivor—trained as a lawyer.

When Bone majored in English literature and Russian at Georgetown University, her mother thought she couldn't make a living with that kind of degree.

"Melanie didn't want to go to medical school. I pushed her for the interview," agrees her mother, Shirley Kaye, who had a hard life growing up and believed her children should be practical. And self-reliant.

Melanie's sister calls their mother a "tough cookie."

"All the kids were on their own," says Kaye. "They had to figure out how to go to college. My husband had to work his way through college as a chef. I don't think it hurt us any. I believe you have to work."

In spite of this, Bone says she "was not a girl who was particularly independent."

She had a brief two-year marriage at 25 during the last year of medical school, grabbing on to steady herself for a move with her residency.

But when she met attorney Bill Bone at 31, their relationship was nothing like her previous one. She was knocked off her feet.

"Bill was a bigger-than-life personality. I'd never been with anything like that in my life," she says. "He sent me two dozen roses, he sent me perfume I saw in the store (on a date) and had it delivered to my door the next day. It was like a fairy tale."

They married in New Zealand in 1992.

They were two bright professionals who lived life in the fast lane, jet-setting around the world and becoming known for supporting charities.

"He's an incredibly philanthropic man," she says.

As the years went on, she had no regrets that she became a doctor. That became especially true after her cancer diagnosis.

"[Cancer] survivors have a very special way of living," she says. "My way of living is, I'm a doctor, and I need to take care of people. There's a true empathy I can feel, and I need to use that for the greater good."

It was her cancer that enabled her to recognize her own worth, she says.

"The more people I helped, the more I started to understand I was kind of an OK person. I am a cool person," she says with a smile behind the desk of her West Palm Beach office in the Bone Building, where she now works part-time.

As she evaluated her sense of self-worth, she decided she wanted a divorce from Bill, her husband of 12 years.

"Maybe what I needed and wanted was different in the long run than what I thought in the short run," she says.

Memories of her illness still haunt

Since the divorce, she and her husband continue to share the office building that bears his name.

They also share custody of their four children—Becky, 12, Carlton, 11, Bailey, 9, and Rex, 8.

The children alternate weeks with their father at the home in Palm Beach they grew up in, and with their mother, at the home she bought in West Palm Beach.

"I wanted to leave the house; it had very bad memories for me (because of) the cancer," she explains.

And the memories were justifiably terrifying.

When she was first diagnosed, she didn't think she would survive. Being a doctor made it worse.

"When I looked at my pathology [report], I definitely thought I was going to die."

It showed a large mass in her left breast.

She had a mastectomy and reconstruction with implants, followed by chemotherapy for six months and radiation for six weeks.

"My last treatment was April 10, 2001. The date is indelible in my brain!"

It was during treatment, she said, that she began to realize that the disease may have brought with it a blessing, a realization of her purpose.

"I had weird things happen to me when I was sick. I'm so scientific by nature, I can't say I have the greatest [religious] belief. For example, I was in bed during chemo, and I shut my eyes, and felt something on my forehead. I thought the kids were playing around. The feeling was, 'You're going to be OK.' I do think somebody was telling me a message: 'Your work on this planet is not done yet. You have to figure out what it is.'

"It was like, I'm on a mission, and I've got to figure out what I'm going to do. From that point forward, my cause found me in life. It was very strong, the pull to help survivors."

'There is no shame' in the journey

Writing about surviving cancer is part of that mission. Though she's a doctor, she still had much to learn about the disease when she struggled through it.

At one point, she wondered whether having four children with almost no pause had flooded her body with estrogen, leading to the cancer—but she later discovered that her father carried the breast cancer gene. She says many people don't know the gene can be passed down this way.

She also admits she needed therapy for the depression that developed with the cancer.

"There is no shame," she says. "When your denial goes away, you can express the depression. I'm not depressed now at all."

Bone is dating a man she met through JDate, an online dating site geared to Jewish couples. Eric Rawet is a widower whose wife died four years ago at 44 of colon cancer.

"He totally gets it," she says, adding that other men she met dropped her when they found out she was a cancer survivor.

With the relationship came the need to confront her feelings about her altered body.

"I think a lot of my fears were probably more in my own head than in reality," she says. "I was pretty open about it. I was scared.

"But I think if you're really attracted to someone emotionally, you figure your way around the physical part."

As for death?

"If it happens, it happens. With cancer, there aren't a lot of unsaid things."

About the Author

Melanie Bone is nationally known for her educational lectures and expertise on the topic of hereditary cancer syndromes. For the past 20 years, Bone has been an obstetrician/gynecologist. She now practices only gynecology, specializing in laparoscopic surgery. As both a doctor and a cancer survivor, she is uniquely qualified to educate professionals and the public about the cancer experience.

Bone graduated from the Phillips Exeter Academy and Georgetown University (Phi Beta Kappa, magna cum laude). She received her medical degree from Albany Medical College, where she was elected to Alpha Omega Alpha, the national medical honors society. Following her obstetrics and gynecologic residency at George Washington University, she practiced in Washington, DC, Northern Virginia, and Maryland. In 1991, Bone moved to Palm Beach, Florida, where she currently maintains her private practice.

Always a go-getter, Bone joined the Florida Obstetric and Gynecologic Society and was slated to become president of this statewide organization when, in August 2000, she was diagnosed with stage III breast cancer at the age of 40. With four children under the age of 5, Bone needed to survive. She decided to make cancer the *best* thing that ever happened to her—and so she has.

Bone is a respected and recognized speaker, writer, and community leader. She was voted as one of the 55 most influential people in Palm Beach County and was given the title of "inspirer." Her popular weekly column, called "Surviving Life," appears in the *Palm Beach Post* and is now syndicated to numerous newspapers across the country. It relates cancer to everyday life and answers cancer-related questions submitted by readers in a "Dear Abby" format. Bone has also founded Cancer Sensibility, a non-profit foundation whose mission is to "put cancer in its place" through educational materials, inspirational speaking, and a website with practical gifts for cancer patients.

Cancer: WHAT NEXT?

Cancer: What Next? is designed to help guide patients, loved ones, and friends through their unique cancer experience. The book describes, each step of the way, what is next in each person's unique path through, and likely beyond, cancer.

TOPICS INCLUDE:

Before Diagnosis
Denial and Anger
Information Seeking
Finding the Right Physician
Treatment Decisions
Alternative Treatments
During Treatment
Family Fallout
Early Survivorship
Late Survivorship
Recurrence
Death
Cancer Etiquette

Melanie Bone is nationally known for her educational lectures and expertise on the topic of hereditary cancer syndromes. For the past 20 years, Bone has been an obstetrician/gynecologist. She now practices only gynecology, specializing in laparoscopic surgery. As both a physician and a cancer survivor, she is uniquely qualified to educate professionals and the public about the cancer experience.

HEALTHY LEARNING™
www.healthylearning.com

ISBN 978-1-60679-111-0

91995

9 781606 791110 $19.95

Dedication

For my four amazing children, Becky, Carlton, Bailey, and Rex, whose love was like a bed of clouds during my illness and who continue to support me and my causes unconditionally.

For my darling husband, Eric, who married me, a cancer survivor, having already lost the mother of his own children to cancer at a tender age. You are brave and my rock. And, you are patient beyond measure, spending nights and weekends organizing this book with me and not complaining about it.

I love you all.

Acknowledgments

My immediate family, Mom, Dad (watching me from above), sister Lori-Nan, and brother Neil helped me considerably by forgiving me periods of remaining incommunicado while working on this project.

Kudos to my office staff, Sabrey, Jennifer, and Lisa, who have kept things running smoothly for me.

Minx Boren, you are a star to help me with the chapter quotes and provide a regular "can do" column for my website.

To Leslie Yanes, my housekeeper of 17 years, a huge hug and kiss for keeping my family safe and cared for while I was attending to my own cancer needs.

Contents

Preface

Some people know me as Dr. Bone, others as Melanie. To four special souls, I am "Mom," and to my husband, I am "Baby." No matter what you call me now, I was just Melanie Bone when my cancer story started back in early 2000.

It was late January, my 40th birthday was just around the corner in February. I noticed a lump in my left armpit when I was showering. Thinking I had cut myself shaving, I took a short course of antibiotics in case I had developed an infection that caused a lymph node to swell. A week later it was still there, but it didn't hurt, so I ignored it. A month later it was still there. At this time, I was training for a marathon, and my children were 2, 3, 4, and 5 years old. With work and a husband, too, I had no time to worry about that silly lump. Eventually, I went for a mammogram and sonogram. The doctor told me they were normal. I again decided to ignore it. That was in April.

In July, the lump was still there. I was feeling a little run down, but chalked it up to stress and a lot of jogging. I was down to 100 pounds. Though people thought I looked "great," I got this nagging sense that something was wrong. Looking into the mirror, I thought I looked sick. I decided to get the lump taken out. I sent the family to Walt Disney World, and I worked all day. Then, I jumped onto the operating room table at 4:30 p.m. At 6 p.m., I woke up to people crying. I knew right away. When they told me I had cancer, I was just confused as to where it was coming from.

The next two days were spent getting scans. The MRI pointed to a small (less than an inch) cancer deep in my left breast near my rib cage.

I met with a cancer specialist and my surgeon. They were happy for me to do whatever I wanted to do. I explained that I was worried about having to go through this all again and wanted to have both my breasts removed. I had to have a mastectomy on the left anyway because of the location of the tumor. As I suspected, the chances of a good reconstruction were best if both sides were done simultaneously. Eight hours of surgery went by in a flash. Before I went to sleep, I had droopy 32As. I woke up with perky mounds about the same size. The recovery was not too bad. I was motivated to be at my daughter's kindergarten party two weeks later. I made it, much to everyone's surprise.